"Fantast Social Studies Lessons Using Literature

for the Media Specialist and Classroom Teacher

by Lynne Farrell Stover

© 2005 Pieces of Learning
CLC0348
ISBN 1-931334-61-7
Graphic Production by Sharolyn Hill

www.piecesoflearning.com

All rights reserved. In our effort to produce high quality educational products we offer portions of this book as "reproducible." Permission is granted, therefore, to the buyer - one teacher - to reproduce student activity pages in LIMITED quantities for students in the buyer's classroom only. The right to reproduce is not extended to other teachers, entire schools, or to school systems. Use of any pages on the Internet is strictly forbidden. No other part of this publication may be reproduced in whole or part. The whole publication may not be stored in a retrieval system, or transmitted in any form or by any means, electronic, mechanical, photocopying, recording, or otherwise without written permission of the publisher.
For any other use contact Pieces of Learning at 1-800-729-5137.
For a complete catalog of products contact Pieces of Learning or visit our Web Site at
www.piecesoflearning.com

Table of Contents

Who Needs This Book? 5
Sample National Standards 6
Introduction 9
Considerations Concerning Teaching the Lessons 10

Economics & Entrepreneurship
Gringotts Bank – *Harry Potter and the Sorcerer's Stone* 12
Goods and Services: Silver Shoes and Flying Monkeys – *The Wizard of Oz* 20
Economic Systems of Middle-earth – *The Lord of the Rings:*
   The Fellowship of the Rings 28
Galleons, Sickles, and Knuts – *Harry Potter and the Prisoner of Azkaban* 37
Charlie's Chocolates – *Charlie and the Chocolate Factory* 44

History & Civics
The Pockets of Presidents – *Gulliver's Travels* 51
Captain Cook & Captain Hook: Fact or Fiction? – *Peter Pan* 57
Mudbloods, Muggles, and Magic: Prejudices in Potter's World –
   Harry Potter and the Order of the Phoenix 63
Pullman's Propaganda: The Power of the Press – *I Was a Rat!* 68
Faun's Flag and Beaver's Banner – *The Lion, the Witch and the Wardrobe* 73

Maps, Graphs & Charts
Make a Map for Milo – *The Phantom Tollbooth* 79
Grid Work: Mapping a Serious Situation – *The Wide Window*
   (A Series of Unfortunate Events) 86
Building Graphs – *Sideways Stories from Wayside School* 92
Codes, Ciphers, and Secret Messages – *The Hostile Hospital*
   (A Series of Unfortunate Events) 98
The Time Warp Trio Time Line – *See You Later, Gladiator*
   (The Time Warp Trio Series) 106

BookList 112

About the Author

Lynne Stover is a Teacher Consultant for the Center on Economic
Education, James Madison University.
She brings her experience to this book as
an author, former media specialist, gifted resource teacher,
social studies teacher, and librarian.
Lynne has been recognized as
The Wilbur S. Pence, Rockingham County Teacher of the Year,
The Virginia Council on Economic Education Teacher of the Year,
The Virginia Association for the Gifted Teacher of the Year
and recipient of
The Business Week/McGraw-Hill Award for Instructional Innovation.

"Who Needs This Book?"
A Poem

Who Needs This Book?

The *gifted resource specialist* is extremely perplexed.
How can he support curriculum beyond the standard text?

The *reading teacher*, desiring to make connections and alliances
Is searching for ways to link literature and the social sciences.

The *classroom teacher*, opportunist and plotter,
Wishes to take advantage of the popular " Mr. Potter."

The *librarian*, while ready, willing, and eager,
Is tied to a schedule in which time is quite meager.

The *social studies teacher* has given serious thought
Of interesting ways economics can be taught.

All these educators are definitely yearning
To teach creatively while addressing standards of learning.

"Fantastic" Social Studies Lessons is just what is looked-for.
To teach quick & fun lessons . . . why ask for more?

Extension activities are included for the precocious.
(Plus lessons have "loopholes" for those who find monsters ferocious.)

Terrific Teachers and Marvelous Media Specialists are sure to find
Skills taught in *"Fantastic" Social Studies Lessons* will enrich the young mind.

Sample National Standards

Lesson	Performance Objectives SOCIAL STUDIES	Standard(s) Curriculum Standards for the Social Studies - NCSS	Performance Objectives LANGUAGE ARTS	Standard(s) Standards for the English Language Arts - NCTE
Gringotts Bank	- Describe how people create that reflect cultural values - Describe how institutional affiliations contribute to personal identity - Demonstrate people's interactions with institutions - Describe institutions in an economic system (specifically banks)	III People, Places, & Environments – g IV Individuals Development & Identity - c V Individuals, Groups, & Institutions – c VII Production, Distribution, & Consumption – d	- Discuss specific role of structured institutions - Follow written instructions	5. Students employ a wide range of strategies as they write and use different writing process elements appropriately to communicate effectively with a variety of purposes. 12. Students use spoken, written, and visual language to accomplish their own purpose.
Goods & Services: Silver Shoes and Flying Monkeys	- Explain the choices concerning goods and services in an economic system - Describe the role of specialization and exchange in an economic system	VII Production, Distribution, & Consumption – a, e	- Use pre knowledge to determine and classify goods and services - Create an outline	1. Students read a wide range of print and nonprint texts to build an understanding of texts, themselves, and of the cultures of the United States and the world; to acquire new information; to respond to the needs and demands of society and the workplace; and for personal fulfillment. Among these texts are fiction and nonfiction, classic and contemporary works.
Economic Systems of Middle-earth	- Explain and illustrate how values and beliefs influence economic decisions - Explain basic economic systems according to who determines what is produced, distributed, and consumed	VII Production, Distribution, & Consumption – f, h	- Discuss the significance of the works of J.R.R. Tolkien - Make connections between an imaginary world and real-life situations - Participate in a creative problem solving activity	2. Students read a wide range of literature from many periods in many genres to build an understanding of the many dimensions (e.g., philosophical, ethical, aesthetic) of the human experience. 11. Students participate as knowledgeable, reflective, creative, and critical members of a variety of literary communities.
Galleons, Sickles, & Knuts	- Discover the role that supply and demand determine in the distribution of goods in a competitive market system - Describe the role of specialization and exchange in the economic process - Differentiate among various forms of exchange and money	VII Production, Distribution, & Consumption – b, e, g	- Use a formatted visual aid to assist in the evaluation of the merits of specific related items - Participate in an interactive activity based on a fictional characterr - Use literary works as tools for research	1. Students read a wide range of print and nonprint texts to build an understanding of texts, themselves, and of the cultures of the United States and the world; to acquire new information; to respond to the needs and demands of society and the workplace; and for personal fulfillment. Among these texts are fiction and nonfiction, classic and contemporary works. 4. Students adjust the use of spoken, written, and visual language (e.g., conversation, style, vocabulary) to communicate effectively with different audiences for a variety of purposes. 11. Students participate as knowledgeable, reflective, creative, and critical members of a variety of literary communities.
Charlie's Chocolates	- Apply knowledge of how groups work to meet individual needs and promote the common good - Discover the role that incentives play in determining what is produced	V Individuals, Groups, & Institutions – g VII Production, Distribution, & Consumption – b	- Participate in a creative problem solving problem - Present a creative solution	4. Students adjust the use of spoken, written, and visual language (e.g., conversation, style, vocabulary) to communicate effectively with different audiences for a variety of purposes 11. Students participate as knowledgeable, reflective, creative, and critical members of a variety of literary communities.

© Pieces of Learning

Sample National Standards

Lesson	Performance Objectives SOCIAL STUDIES	Standard(s) Curriculum Standards for the Social Studies - NCSS	Performance Objectives LANGUAGE ARTS	Standard(s) Standards for the English Language Arts - NCTE
The Pocket of Presidents	- Give examples of how artifacts contribute to the traditions and values of a culture - Identify and describe the basic features of a United States President	I Culture – c VI Power, Authority, & Governance	- Answer questions based on research and pre knowledge	1. Students read a wide range of print and nonprint texts to build an understanding of texts, themselves, and of the cultures of the United States and the world; to acquire new information; to respond to the needs and demands of society and the workplace; and for personal fulfillment. Among these texts are fiction and nonfiction, classic and contemporary works
Captain Cook & Captain Hook: Fact or Fiction?	- Describe instances in which language can facilitate understanding or cause misunderstanding	IX Global Connections – a	- Define and employ the concepts of fact and fiction	3. Students apply a wide range of strategies to comprehend, interpret, evaluate, and appreciate texts.
Mudbloods, Muggles, & Magic: Prejudices In Potter's World	- Compare similarities and differences in groups - Develop empathy and skepticism regarding attitudes and values - Identify examples of stereotyping, conformity, and altruism	I Culture – a, b, e II Time, Continuity, & Change – e, f IV Individual Development & Identity – g, h	- Participate in a class discussion - Research and present specific information	2. Students read a wide range of literature from many periods in many genres to build an understanding of the many dimensions (e.g., philosophical, ethical, aesthetic) of the human experience. 7. Students conduct research in issues and interests by generating ideas and questions, and by posing problems. They gather, evaluate, and synthesize data from a variety of sources (e.g., print and nonprint, texts, artifacts, people) to communicate the discoveries in ways that suit their purpose and audience.
Pullman's Propaganda: The Power of the Press	- Demonstrate an understanding that the same event may be described in different ways	II Time, Continuity, & Change – a	- Complete a chart using specific information - Evaluate types of persuasive writing	1. Students read a wide range of print and nonprint texts to build an understanding of texts, themselves, and of the cultures of the United States and the world; to acquire new information; to respond to the needs and demands of society and the workplace; and for personal fulfillment. Among these texts are fiction and nonfiction, classic and contemporary works. 3. Students apply a wide range of strategies to comprehend, interpret, evaluate, and appreciate texts.
Faun's Flag and Beaver's Banner	- Describe the role of technology in communication and information-processing - Examine and describe the influence of culture on the technological choices and advancement	VI Power, Authority, & Governance – g VIII Science, Technology, & Society – a	- Review literary and visual symbols - Create a unique project using specific information	1. Students read a wide range of print and nonprint texts to build an understanding of texts, themselves, and of the cultures of the United States and the world; to acquire new information; to respond to the needs and demands of society and the workplace; and for personal fulfillment. Among these texts are fiction and nonfiction, classic and contemporary works. 3. Students apply a wide range of strategies to comprehend, interpret, evaluate, and appreciate texts.

© Pieces of Learning

Sample National Standards

Lesson	Performance Objectives SOCIAL STUDIES	Standard(s) Curriculum Standards for the Social Studies - NCSS	Performance Objectives LANGUAGE ARTS	Standard(s) Standards for the English Language Arts - NCTE
Make a Map for Milo	- Elaborate mental maps of locals and regions - Create and use representations of the earth, such as maps	III People, Places & Environments – a, b	- Review and create a map following specific written instructions	3. Students apply a wide range of strategies to comprehend, interpret, evaluate, and appreciate texts. 7. Students conduct research in issues and interests by generating ideas and questions, and by posing problem. They gather, evaluate, and synthesize data from a variety of sources (e.g., print and nonprint, texts, artifacts, people) to communicate the discoveries in ways that suit their purpose and audience.
Grid Work: Mapping a Serious Situation	- Create and use representations of the earth, such as maps - Estimate distance and calculate scale	III People, Places & Environments – b, d	- Review and create a map following specific written instructions	3. Students apply a wide range of strategies to comprehend, interpret, evaluate, and appreciate texts. 7. Students conduct research in issues and interests by generating ideas and questions, and by posing problem. They gather, evaluate, and synthesize data from a variety of sources (e.g., print and nonprint, texts, artifacts, people) to communicate the discoveries in ways that suit their purpose and audience.
Building Graphs	- Use data sources to create graphs and charts	III People, Places & Environments – c	- Review the characteristics of visual data and its importance in revealing factual data - Read and interpret provided information to create visual data	3. Students apply a wide range of strategies to comprehend, interpret, evaluate, and appreciate texts. 7. Students conduct research in issues and interests by generating ideas and questions, and by posing problems. They gather, evaluate, and synthesize data from a variety of sources (e.g., print and nonprint, texts, artifacts, people) to communicate the discoveries in ways that suit their purpose and audience.
Codes, Ciphers, and Secret Messages	- Use appropriate data sources to interpret information	III People, Places & Environments – c	- Review and discuss the characteristics and historical significance of codes - Participate in decoding and encoding	3. Students apply a wide range of strategies to comprehend, interpret, evaluate, and appreciate texts. 7. Students conduct research in issues and interests by generating ideas and questions, and by posing problem. They gather, evaluate, and synthesize data from a variety of sources (e.g., print and nonprint, texts, artifacts, people) to communicate the discoveries in ways that suit their purpose and audience.
The Time Warp Trio Time Line	- Use processes important to reconstructing the past - Use facts and concepts drawn from history - Use data sources to create graphs and charts	II Time, Continuity & Change – d, f III People, Places & Environments – c	- Discuss historical fiction - Create a timeline	1. Students read a wide range of print and nonprint texts to build an understanding of texts, themselves, and of the cultures of the United States and the world; to acquire new information; to respond to the needs and demands of society and the workplace; and for personal fulfillment. Among these texts are fiction and nonfiction, classic and contemporary works. 2. Students apply a wide range of strategies to comprehend, interpret, evaluate, and appreciate texts.

© Pieces of Learning

Introduction

Everyone loves a good story. For librarians, reading specialists, language arts teachers, and gifted education coordinators, making use of literature to teach economics, civics, and geography lessons can be a sensible strategy for many reasons. One of the major motivations for combining the two disciplines is that students can relate to a well-known and much loved piece of literature when integrated into a skill most often taught within the social sciences. An activity concerning the attributes of money and its application when applied to the exchange of goods and services using Harry Potter's Galleons, Sickles, and Knuts is far more interesting than using everyday currency. Most agree it is much more interesting to learn about map grids using an imaginary island and propaganda techniques when Cinderella's rat-turned-page is involved.

Just as important is the fact that an interdisciplinary approach to instruction becomes a necessity as educators deal with a jam-packed curriculum. By combining literature with social studies activities it is possible to get "more bang for the buck." Also, by combining economics with literature, history with artistic creativity, and graphs and charts with math skills, students are able to make connections in what they are learning. (It is often the lack of these connections that make the whole educational process very frustrating for struggling learners, gifted students, and all those in between.)

Also of consideration is the knowledge that a lesson using literature to teach a social studies concept makes it possible for support personal, such as librarians, reading specialists, and gifted education teachers, to augment classroom instruction. In times when it is necessary for resource teachers to validate their usefulness in the educational process and to promote the significant role they play in student learning and curriculum support, teaching outside an area of expertise is definitely a good idea.

Considerations Concerning Teaching the Lessons

The fifteen lessons included in this book are appropriate for students in upper elementary and middle school; however, they may be adapted for younger or older students. The lessons need not be taught in sequence, as each one stands alone. With a few exceptions, when it might be necessary for a teacher to continue the activity in the classroom, the lessons can be taught in a 30-45-minute time frame.

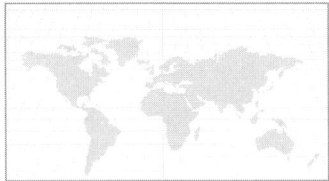

Each lesson opens with a **quote** by a character or a **passage** by the author of the featured fantasy book. These "insights" provide a connection between the selected pieces of literature and the social studies lesson. They are for the teacher's edification. These quotes may be shared with the students to set the tone, but they have not been incorporated within the lesson itself.

A provided **synopsis** helps the teacher recall the basic content of the story. Note that while the literature selected includes titles from children's classics to contemporary best sellers, it is not necessary for all of the students to have read the selected pieces. However, as many have been made into feature films, most students will be familiar with the characters, settings, and plots.

The **content connection** validates the choice of a book as the appropriate tie-in to the social studies skill being addressed.

The **stated objectives** are general in nature and can easily be restated to apply to most curriculum content or mandated standards of learning.

The **materials** listed are minimal. In most cases, an overhead projector for the transparencies, a water-soluble pen, the ability to mass produce an activity sheet, and some paper and pencils will be all that is required.

The **lessons** include visuals and activity sheets.

 The **visuals** are designated with this icon so that they may be made into transparencies to be used with an overhead projector. However, if an overhead projector is not available, the information on the visuals may be reproduced on a chalk board or chart paper.

The **activity sheets** are indicated with this icon and serve several purposes. If the activity is a student worksheet, it will be necessary to duplicate the needed copies prior to class time. If the activity sheet is a component of a game or simulation, preparation time prior to the lesson is also required.

Each lesson includes an **evaluation**. The evaluation is usually subjective. Its purpose is to give the teacher an idea of how well the students have mastered the concept taught and to validate the lesson's importance in the curriculum.

An **extension** indicated with this icon can be found in every lesson. This added activity could also be considered enrichment. Whereas the lessons have been developed for entire class instruction, the extensions are usually for independent learners who have the time and desire to go beyond the regular lesson. Extensions can also be incorporated into effective learning centers.

The excitement and escapism of fantasy literature has captured the interest of many young people. However, it should be noted that not every student has read (or is allowed to read) the fantasy books associated with these lessons. This was considered when the lessons were developed.

It is not necessary to have read the books to successfully complete the activities. There are also some built in "loopholes" for students who feel uncomfortable with the magic and imagination that are such an enchanting part of these books.

Economics & Enterpreneurship

Gringotts Bank

"Enter, stranger, but take heed
Of what awaits the sin of greed,
For those who take, but do not earn,
Must pay most dearly in their turn."

- Inscription on the doors of Gringotts Bank
Harry Potter and the Sorcerer's Stone

Harry Potter and the Sorcerer's Stone
By J.K. Rowling

STORY SYNOPSIS

It is only when young Harry Potter is invited to enroll in Hogwarts School of Witchcraft and Wizardry does he discover he is a wizard. Defying his cruel uncle's wishes, he leaves for Hogwarts under the watchful eye of his mentor, Rubeus Hagrid. At Hogwarts he befriends Ron Weasley and Hermione Granger, attends fascinating classes, encounters bizarre creatures, and discovers someone is trying to steal a magical stone. This powerful stone could bring wicked Lord Voldemort, the wizard who left him parentless and scared, back to power. Harry and his friends foil Voldemort's evil attempt. Because of their bravery, intelligence, and loyalty they win special awards and thus earn the yearly house cup for Gryffindor House.

CONTENT CONNECTION

Hagrid and Harry's first stop before catching the train to Hogwarts School of Witchcraft and Wizardry is the magical market place, Diagon Alley, where he can find all the school supplies that are on his school material's list. Much to his surprise Harry discovers that his parents left him a fortune in wizard world money in a vault at the goblin-controlled bank, Gringotts. Harry may be wealthy in the world of magic, but he realizes that the currency of the magical realm, Galleons, Sickles, and Knuts, has no value in the "Muggle" world.

Harry quickly learns other interesting information about the culture of which he is becoming a member. It appears that even in a society of charms and enchantments, money is still an important tool in facilitating the exchange of goods and services. The wizards have their own unique currency and banking system that plays a significant role in their magical world.

TIME REQUIRED: 30 minutes

© Pieces of Learning

Economics & Enterpreneurship

Gringotts Bank

OBJECTIVES
- The student will be introduced to (or review) banking and check writing.
- The student will participate in a class discussion concerning the concept of withdrawing funds from an account to purchase goods and services.
- The student may participate in the extension activity dealing with the research of a related topic.

MATERIALS
- Visuals - **Potter's Personal Purchases** (p.16) and **Does Your Check Look Like This?** (p.17)
- Water soluble marker
- Activity - **Check Writing Practice & Banking Discussion Questions** (p.18-19) - a copy for each student or group

PROCEDURE

1. Tell the students that today's lesson will deal with banks and the services they provide. Ask the students if anyone remembers the name of the bank in the Harry Potter series. [*Gringotts Bank*] Ask students if they can recall some unique characteristics about this fictional bank. [Possible answers: *Goblins run it. There are branches all over the world. The vaults are deep underground. Dragons guard the vaults*]

2. Display Visual - **Potter's Personal Purchases**

3. Explain to the students that one of the services that a bank provides is that of allowing the customer to maintain a checking account. Checks may be written to the bank, and the bank in turn will withdraw money from the account to pay the person or business to whom the check was written. The displayed visual is an example of what a check written by Harry Potter might look like.

4. Solicit student responses to the questions on the visual and record the replies.
   ANSWERS:
   (1) To whom is the check written? *Flourish and Blotts - A bookstore in Diagon Alley*
   (2) What is written on the memo line? *School Books*
   (3) How many checks were written before this one? *Three. This must be a new account.*
   (4) What do you think the symbol "G" stands for? *Magical Money or Galleons are possible answers.*
   (5) On what date was this check written? *August 1, 1991*

   For Discussion: What are the advantages of writing a check for goods and services?
   Possible answers:
   > You do not need to carry around a lot of heavy money if you have a checkbook.
   > If you lose money it is probably gone forever, but you may get your checkbook back because your name is on it.
   > You can keep a record of what you spend.

Economics & Enterpreneurship
Gringotts Bank

What are the disadvantages of writing checks?
Possible answers:
> You can overdraw your account if you do not keep good records.
> If you lose your checkbook and a dishonest person finds it, you could be in big trouble!

Why is the amount of the check written in both numerals and words?
Possible answers:
> To double check the amount. If the numbers are sloppy, the banker could see what the words say. Numbers are easy to change, but someone would have a harder time changing words.

Why is the signature an important and necessary part of a check?
Possible answers:
> It is a means of identification.
> It proves who is withdrawing the money.

What do you think the coded numbers on the bottom of the check are?
Possible answers:
> Numbers that the bank uses to identify a specific account.
> Special numbers so the bank can tell you really have an account with them.
> Something to keep people with the same names from getting their checking accounts mixed up.

5. Pass out Activity 1 - **Check Writing Practice & Banking Discussion Questions Part I and II**. Allow the students ten minutes to work on the worksheet. They may work individually or in groups.

6. Check for understanding by displaying the filled in check on the visual **Does Your Check Look Like This?** Record the students' responses to the discussion questions on the visual. (Possible answers appear in the EVALUATION section of the lesson plan.)

EVALUATION

What services do you think a bank provides?

> Possible answers: *Banks provide: Savings Accounts, Check Cashing, Checking Accounts, Loans, Travelers Checks*

How does a bank make money?

> Possible answers: *Charging Interest on Loans, Charging fees for Services, Interest on Investments*

Why is it necessary for a bank to have a security system?

> Possible answers: *The bank must have the trust of the customers. An alarm system and security guards help protect the bank from robbers.*

Economics & Enterpreneurship

Gringotts Bank

EXTENSION

Dragon Defense Department

There is a rumor that the goblins at Gringotts Bank use dragons to guard the underground vaults. To prove this to be true, a person would need to do some investigative research. Pick one of the topics below and find three <u>different</u> reference tools that contain information about it. (Examples: An encyclopedia, an Internet cite, a magazine article, a non fiction book or a television documentary program.) List ten interesting facts about your topic. Be prepared to share your finding with the class.

- Famous Bank Robbers or Bank Robberies
- Banking During the Middle Ages
- Counterfeit Money
- The History of Check Writing
- Security in Financial Institutions
- Your Choice (Teacher Approval Required)

© Pieces of Learning

Economics & Enterpreneurship

Gringotts Bank

Potter's Personal Purchases

Questions

1. To whom is the check written? _____

2. What is written on the Memo line? _____

3. How many checks were written before this one? _____

4. What do you think the symbol "☪" stands for? _____

5. On what date was this check written? _____

For Discussion

What are the advantages of writing a check for goods and services?

What are the disadvantages of writing checks?

Why is the amount of the check written in both numerals and words?

Why is the signature an important and necessary part of a check?

What do you think the coded numbers on the bottom of the check are?

16 © Pieces of Learning

Economics & Enterpreneurship

Gringotts Bank

Does Your Check Look Like This?

```
Pat Pupil                                           NO. 45
123 Perfect Place                                   Date: 8/31/05
Somewhere, USA.

Pay to the order of: _____Smart Student Store_____   $ 13.50
       Thirteen and 50/100 ——————                        Dollars
           Somewhere Bank

Memo  School Supplies                              Pat Pupil

00008200'oooo::15 • 0045
```

What are some possible answers to the questions below?

1. What services do you think a bank provides?

2. How does a bank make money?

3. Why is it necessary for a bank to have a security system?

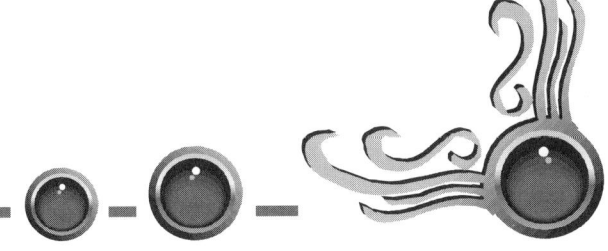

Economics & Enterpreneurship

Gringotts Bank

Name: _____

Check Writing Practice
&
Banking Discussion Questions

PART I

```
_____                                    NO. _____
_____                                    Date: _____
_____

Pay to the order of _____  $_____

_____Dollars
Somewhere Bank


Memo_____    _____

 • 00008200'oooo::15 •  0045
```

Use the following information to fill in the above check:

- The account holder is Pat Pupil, of 123 Perfect Place, Somewhere, USA.
- The date is August 31, 2005.
- Pat is purchasing $13.50 worth of school supplies at the Smart Student Store.
- Pat has used 44 checks before this one.

Economics & Enterpreneurship

Gringotts Bank

PART II

Be prepared to discuss the following questions.
Make notes in the space provided.

What services do you think a bank provides?

How does a bank make money?

Why is it necessary for a bank to have a security system?

Economics & Enterpreneurship

Goods and Services: Silver Shoes and Flying Monkeys

"Many shops stood in the street, and Dorothy saw that everything in them was green. Green candy and green popcorn were offered for sale, as well as green shoes and green hats and green clothes of all sorts. At one place a man was selling green lemonade, and when the children bought it Dorothy could see that they paid for it with green pennies."

- A Description of the Shops in the Emerald City
The Wonderful Wizard of OZ

The Wonderful Wizard of OZ
By L. Frank Baum

STORY SYNOPSIS

Dorothy and her dog, Toto, find they have been transported to the magical Land of Oz when a cyclone hits her Kansas home. Upon landing, she discovers she is indirectly responsible for the death of the Wicked Witch of the East. Taking the recently departed witch's silver shoes she decides to seek help in her quest to return home. Alone and confused she soon befriends a Scarecrow, a Tin Woodman, and a Cowardly Lion. The four join forces to find the Great Wizard of Oz, hoping he can help them with their individual problems. The wizard turns out to be less than helpful. However, they receive aid from the unique citizens of the Land of Oz as they have one adventure after another. Eventually the main characters get their "heart's desire" and all their problems are resolved.

CONTENT CONNECTION

The Land of Oz is an interesting place to visit. The inhabitants are unique and the social structure is complex. However different the rules of their society are, the citizens of Oz still prosper by providing goods and services to others.

TIME REQUIRED: 30 minutes.

OBJECTIVES
- The student will define goods and services.
- The student will participate in a sorting and organizing activity.
- The student may participate in the extension activity dealing with the selection of specific goods and services.

© Pieces of Learning

Economics & Enterpreneurship

Goods and Services: Silver Shoes and Flying Monkeys

MATERIALS
- Visual – **Goods and Services in the Land of Oz** (p.23)
- Visual - **Goods and Services: Organizing Oz Answer Sheet** (p.27)
- A water-soluble marker
- Activity - **Identify Consumer, Producer, Good, or Service** (p.24)
- Activity - **Organizing Oz** (p.25-26)
- Scissors and glue sticks or tape for each student or group

PROCEDURE
1. Prepare and collect materials prior to class.

2. Inform the students that the lesson today will deal with economics.

3. Introduce the lesson by displaying the visual **Goods and Services in the Land of Oz**. Read the definitions to the students.

4. Read each item listed and solicit responses. Answers:
   - Dorothy from Kansas - Consumer
   - Oil Can - Good
   - Tin Woodman - Consumer
   - Cowardly Lion's Hair Cut - Service
   - Silver Slippers – Good
   - Tinsmith - Producer
   - Stuffing Straw in the Scarecrow's head - Service
   - Green Tinted Eye Glasses - Good
   - Basket full of Fruit and Nuts - Goods
   - Guarding the Gates of the Emerald City – Service
   - A collar and leash for Toto – Good

5. Pass the two activity sheets to the students. (They may work individually or in groups.) Each student or group will need scissors and glue or tape. Tell the students that you are performing a **service** by passing out **goods** they, as **consumers**, will need to complete the activity.

6. Read these instructions to the class. *"The sentence strips below represent two main ideas related to one topic. Cut out the strips, organize them, and glue them to the appropriate place on the accompanying sheet."*

7. Ask if there are questions and clarify any confusion. Allow the students about ten minutes to complete the activity.

8. Check for understanding.

© Pieces of Learning

Economics & Enterpreneurship

Goods and Services: Silver Shoes and Flying Monkeys

EVALUATION

The correct placement of the sentence strips may be found on the visual check sheet, **Goods and Services: Organizing Oz**. It is not necessary for the sentences on the students' worksheets to appear in the exact order they do on the visual, as long as they are grouped under the correct topics.

Note: There may be several students who will point out a mistake in the factual content of the sentences. They will tell you that Dorothy's slippers were red instead of silver. Explain to them that they were silver in the book and ask why they think the maker of the movie took the liberty to make them red. (Be prepared for some interesting theories!)

EXTENSION

Challenge the students with the following activity:

Planning a Trip?

Dorothy's trip to the Land of Oz was unexpected and she did not have time to prepare for it. If you were planning to visit Oz what GOODS and SERVICES would you need for the journey? Create a list of at least ten goods you would take and ten services you would utilize prior to reaching your final destination. If you need help, you may use the yellow pages in the phone book to help you generate some ideas.

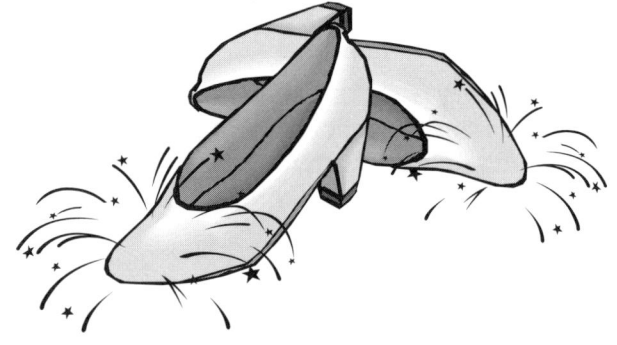

Economics & Enterpreneurship

Goods and Services: Silver Shoes and Flying Monkeys

Goods and Services in the Land of Oz

Definitions

A **CONSUMER** is a person who uses GOODS and SERVICES to satisfy wants and needs.

A **PRODUCER** is an individual or group that makes a good and/or provides a service.

A **GOOD** is a tangible item that consumers want. In other words, it is something that can be touched or held.

A **SERVICE** is an activity that satisfies a consumer's want. In other words, it is something that is done for someone else.

© Pieces of Learning

Economics & Enterpreneurship

Goods and Services: Silver Shoes and Flying Monkeys

Identify **CONSUMER, PRODUCER, GOOD** or **SERVICE**

Dorothy from Kansas _____

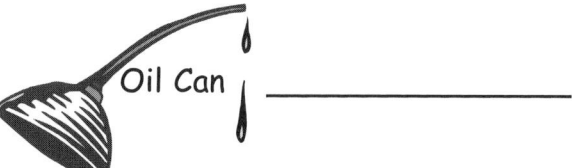

Oil Can _____

Tin Woodman _____

Cowardly Lion's Hair Cut _____

Silver Slippers _____

Tinsmith _____

Stuffing Straw in the Scarecrow's head _____

Green Tinted Eye Glasses _____

Basket full of Fruit and Nuts

_____

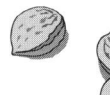

Guarding the Gates of the Emerald City _____

A collar and leash for Toto _____

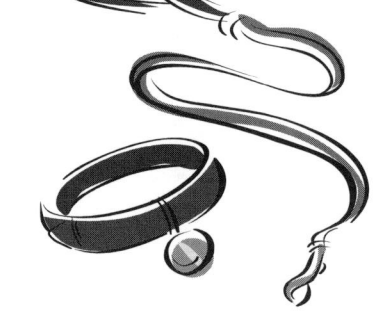

Economics & Enterpreneurship

Goods and Services: Silver Shoes and Flying Monkeys

Organizing Oz

The sentence strips below represent two main ideas related to one topic. Cut out the strips, organize them, and glue them to the appropriate place on the accompanying sheet. (The title has been listed; just paste the correct strip over it!)

--------- The Winkie tinsmiths repaired the damaged Tin Woodman. ---------

--------- The Golden Cap Dorothy was wearing was magic and allowed its owner three wishes. ---------

--------- The field mice joined forces and rolled the sleeping lion out of the poppy field. ---------

--------- The Tin Woodman's gold handled ax was a great improvement over his old one. ---------

--------- Goods and services available only in the Land of Oz helped Dorothy return to Kansas. ---------

--------- Dorothy and her friends received some unique services while traveling through Oz. ---------

--------- The Winged Monkeys flew the four friends back to Oz. ---------

--------- The silver slippers Dorothy wore held the secret to her returning home. ---------

--------- Some extraordinary goods helped the four friends in their travels through Oz. ---------

© Pieces of Learning

25

Economics & Enterpreneurship

Goods and Services: Silver Shoes and Flying Monkeys

Name:_____

Goods and Services
Organizing Oz

Title

| Goods and services available only in the Land of Oz helped Dorothy return to Kansas. |

First Main Topic

| |

Supporting Detail 1

| |

Supporting Detail 2

| |

Supporting Detail 3

| |

Second Main Topic

| |

Supporting Detail 1

| |

Supporting Detail 2

| |

Supporting Detail 3

| |

© Pieces of Learning

Economics & Enterpreneurship

Goods and Services: Silver Shoes and Flying Monkeys

Goods and Services
Organizing Oz - Answer Sheet

Title
Goods and services available only in the Land of Oz helped Dorothy return to Kansas.

First Main Topic
Some extraordinary goods helped the four friends in their travels through Oz.

Supporting Detail 1
The silver slippers Dorothy wore held the secret to her returning home.

Supporting Detail 2
The Tin Woodman's gold handled ax was a great improvement over his old one.

Supporting Detail 3
The Golden Cap Dorothy was wearing was magic and allowed its owner three wishes.

Second Main Topic
Dorothy and her friends received some unique services while traveling through Oz.

Supporting Detail 1
The Winged Monkeys flew the four friends back to Oz.

Supporting Detail 2
The field mice joined forces and rolled the sleeping lion out of the poppy field.

Supporting Detail 3
The Winkie tinsmiths repaired the damaged Tin Woodman.

© Pieces of Learning

Economics & Enterpreneurship

Economic Systems of Middle-earth

"Bilbo was very rich and very peculiar, and had been the wonder of the Shire for sixty years, ever since his remarkable disappearance and unexpected return. The riches he had brought back from his travels had now become a local legend, and it was popularly believed, whatever the old folk might say, the Hill at Bag End was full of tunnels stuffed with treasure."

- Introduction in Chapter I
The Fellowship of the Ring

The Lord of the Rings:
The Fellowship of the Ring
By J.R.R. Tolkien

STORY SYNOPSIS

The date was September 22nd and Bilbo Baggins, the hero of *The Hobbit,* and his young relative, Frodo, were celebrating their joint birthdays. It is during the well-planned festivities that Bilbo, now one hundred eleven years old, makes a grand exit, disappearing in front of all his guests. Thus starts the tale of Frodo who later, at fifty years of age, would leave the comforts of his home in the Shire and assume the role of "Ring Bearer."

Frodo learns about the ring he has inherited from Bilbo from Gandalf the Grey, a powerful wizard. When told the ring in question was forged thousands of years ago and is evil incardinate, Frodo realizes it must be destroyed. Sam the gardener, and two young relatives, Merry and Pippin, accompany Frodo on this quest. Along the way they are joined by Strider, a ranger, hunted by Ringwraiths, and saved by Elves. It is while Frodo is recuperating with the Elves that the "Fellowship of the Ring" is formed. The four hobbits are joined by two men, Aragon and Boromir, Gimli a Dwarf, an Elf, Legolas and Gandalf. As the group travels to Mordor, the ring's place of origin, they are attacked by orcs and lose Gandalf to the monster, Durin's Bane. After a respite in the elfin land of Lothioien the group sets out in elfin boats down the Great River. It is at a resting place that Frodo realizes he must continue alone on his errand of death. However, the faithful Sam would not allow his master to travel without him. The two hobbits continue down the river on their own.

The story continues with the next book in the trilogy, *The Two Towers.*

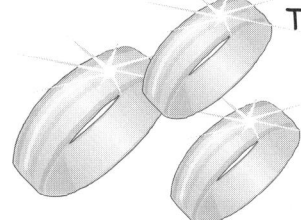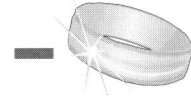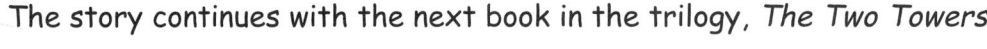

Economics & Enterpreneurship
Economic Systems of Middle-earth

CONTENT CONNECTION
The Lord of the Rings trilogy was written in an era of global unrest when nations were seeking economic growth while establishing the role they were to play in the political arena. Was *The Fellowship of the Ring* written as an analogy of that time? J.R.R. Tolkien may have been describing communism when writing of the dark and desolate Mordor and predicting World War II when referring to the coming of the great darkness. The elves of Rivendell could be compared to the future allied forces. The wholesome innocence of the hobbits of the Shire may be representing bucolic rural England.

(The relationship between the brave and steadfast gardener Sam Gamgee and the wealthy Frodo Baggins was defiantly a statement concerning the interdependence of the members of the British class system.)

TIME REQUIRED: 30-40 minutes.

OBJECTIVES
- The student will be introduced to (or review) Traditional, Command, Market, and Mixed Economic systems.
- The students will review the concept of completing analogies and participate in an activity dealing with economic concepts.
- The student may participate in the extension activity dealing with the allocation of limited resources and creative problem solving.

MATERIALS
- Visual - **What is an Economic System?** (p.32)
- Activity - **Economic Systems of Middle-earth** (p.33)
- Activity - **Analogy Worksheet** (p.34)
- Optional – Extension Visual - **Buckley Brandybuck's Birthday Bash Dilemma** (p.35) and Activity - **Buckley's Birthday Bash Dilemma** (p.36)

PROCEDURE
1. Ask the students if they are familiar with the books of J.R.R Tolkien, *The Hobbit* and *The Lord of the Rings Trilogy*. Explain that when Tolkien wrote these tales of adventure and good overcoming evil he created a complex imaginary world. In this world there lived peaceful hobbits, wise elves, warring men, and evil ogres.

    Tolkien created new languages, landscapes, and histories for his characters. Each of the different cultures also had a unique economic system that can be compared to the systems that exist today.

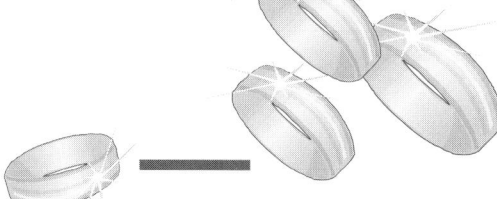

© Pieces of Learning

Economics & Enterpreneurship

Economic Systems of Middle-earth

2. Display the visual - **What is an Economic System?** Read and discuss the information with the class. Examples of countries that "fit" the definitions could be: Traditional – Ethiopia and Bangladesh; Command – Cuba and North Korea; Market – United States, Australia, and Japan. (In reality all economies are mixed. The United States is primarily a Market Economy, but bartering still takes place. and there are some goods and services that are totally regulated by the government.)

3. Distribute the activity – **Economic Systems of Middle-earth**. Read the directions to the students. The students may work individually or in small groups. (This activity sheet may be made into a transparency allowing instruction to be conducted as a class activity.)

4. Allow five minutes to complete the activity. Check for understanding. Answers:
   1. *Market Economy*   2. *Traditional Economy*   3. *Command Economy*
   4. *Market Economy*

5. Distribute the activity **Economic Systems of Middle-earth Analogy Worksheet**. Review analogies with the students by reading the directions at the top of the page. *The students should be able to supply the missing word in the analogy finger : hand :: toe : <u>FOOT</u>*

6. Allow ten minutes to complete this activity. Check for understanding. Answers:
   1. Command Economy   2. Money   3. Bank   4. Market Economy   5. Good
   6. Barter   7. Scarce   8. Taxes

EVALUATION
At the conclusion ask the students to put their heads down on their desks and answer the following questions by raising their right hand if the answer is true and their left hand if the answer is false.

The United States has a market economy. (T)
Most economic systems can be described as being mixed. (T)
Traditional economies are bad and never work well. (F)
I now have a better understanding of Economic Systems (T or F)

EXTENSION
The activity **Buckley Brandybuck's Birthday Bash Dilemma** contains scenario and solution activity sheets that can be found on pages 35 and 36. This activity is ideal for an advanced group of students who enjoy problem-solving challenges and works very well when teacher directed. While there is no one solution to poor Buckley's problem, some students will enjoy debating the best course of action he should take. The economic situations of scarcity, opportunity, cost, and trade-offs all come into play as students try to help Buckley. (Possible student responses are recorded on page 31.)

© Pieces of Learning

Economics & Enterpreneurship

Economic Systems of Middle-earth

What is Buckley Brandybuck's major scarcity problem? *He was suffering from a lack of income because his cabbage crop had failed. There is a limited amount of Hobbits he can invite to his birthday party.*

What are some possible problems with the solutions suggested by Buckley's family members?

(1) **His wife's suggestion- only to invite the wealthy** - *The rich people may be boring. Just because you invite them doesn't mean that they will return the favor. Rich people expect nicer gifts and are harder to please than the less wealthy. The trade-off for inviting only the rich might be a very boring party.*

(2) **His son's suggestion – conduct a lottery** - *Some of your best friends could be left out. You could end up with a group of only the very old or only the very young. (Therefore there could be a scarcity of baby-sitters.) Not all members of the same family may get invited, causing hard feelings.*

(3) **His uncle's suggestion – skip the party** - *This would be NO fun. The cost of skipping the party would be too high. You may not be invited to anyone else's party. In a traditional economy this just is not the way things are done.*

(4) **His sister's suggestion – first come/first serve** - *The closest neighbors have an unfair advantage. The first hobbits may fill all the spaces up with the names of their friends. (They then may barter their invitations to another Hobbit who may have something to trade but lived too far away to get to the house before the invitations list had been filled.)*

What do you think is the best solution for Buckley's problem? Describe how you think he should allocate the invitation's to his party in such a manner as not to suffer too much socially or economically. *Buckley may be able to **benefit** socially by having a smaller Birthday Party, making it a very elite affair. He might save lots of money by giving his guests gift certificates for cabbages from next year's harvest.*

A Gift Certificate for You!

_____

_____

_____

Economics & Enterpreneurship

Economic Systems of Middle-earth

What is an Economic System?

Every society, prosperous or poor, has an economic system. This is because it is always necessary for a society to determine how scarce resources will be allocated.

Economic Systems need to answer these questions:

What Goods and Services to Produce? *What are the needs and wants?*
How to Produce Goods and Services? *What resources should be used?*
For Whom to Produce Goods and Services? *Who receives the products?*

Economic Systems Defined

TRADITIONAL ECONOMY: Decisions about scarce resources are made the way that they have always been made.

COMMAND ECONOMY: A Central authority owns and decides what to do with scare resources.

MARKET ECONOMY: Individuals own and decide what to so with scarce resources. Prices guide economic decisions.

MIXED ECONOMY: In reality, no economy is purely traditional, command, or market. Economies contain characteristics of all three; however, one will be dominant.

© Pieces of Learning

Economics & Enterpreneurship

Economic Systems of Middle-earth

Economic Systems of Middle-earth

Directions: Read each statement. Decide which type of economic system best fits with the situation. Write your answer in the blank. Be prepared to discuss and defend your answers.

> **TRADITIONAL ECONOMY:** Decisions about scarce resources are made the "old fashioned" way.
> **COMMAND ECONOMY:** A central authority owns and decides what to do with scare resources.
> **MARKET ECONOMY:** Individuals own and decide what to do with scarce resources.

1. Because of an increase in demand, the metal master elves of Rivendell increase production on magical axes for the dwarfs who will purchase them for many gold pieces.

    _____

2. Just as their fathers and uncles had done many years before, Merry and Pippin worked in farmer Took's cabbage patch in exchange for a good meal and all the cabbages they could carry home.

    _____

3. The wicked Sauron has taken over all of the factories and ordered all the workers to make swords and helmets for the soldiers of Mordor.

    _____

4. In Hobbiton it is possible to purchase vegetables, shoes, toys, and books from the shop owners on the main road.

    _____

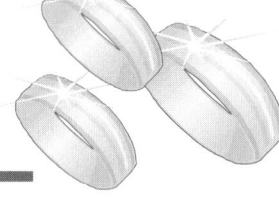

© Pieces of Learning

Economics & Enterpreneurship

Economic Systems of Middle-earth

Analogy Worksheet

An analogy is a correlation in which different things are compared item by item usually with the idea of explaining something unfamiliar by comparing it to something well known.

Analogies are often written in this form:
a:b :: c:d (this is read as, a is to b as c is to d)

EXAMPLES: Frodo is to Hobbit as Legolas is to Elf
Sunshine : Day :: Moonlight : Night
Finger : Hand :: Toe : _____?

Directions: Using the words listed below, complete each analogy. A Word Bank has been provided.

1. USA : Market Economy :: Cuba : _____

2. Read : Words :: Spend : _____

3. Spend : Store :: Save : _____

4. Customary : Traditional Economy :: Innovation : _____

5. Haircut : Service :: Shampoo : _____

6. Sell : Money :: Swap : _____

7. Abundance : Plenty :: Not Enough : _____

8. Business : Revenue :: Government : _____

Word Bank

Bank	Market Economy
Barter	Money
Command Economy	Scarce
Good	Taxes

34

© Pieces of Learning

Economics & Enterpreneurship
Economic Systems of Middle-earth

Buckley Brandybuck's Birthday Bash Dilemma
Scenario

Bilbo Baggins, a very well traveled hobbit, was able to hold a magnificent celebration on his "eleventy-first" birthday. However, his less wealthy relative, Buckley Brandybuck, was not so fortunate. Limited in space and money, Buckley had to make some decisions.

Hobbits celebrate birthdays in grand style. It is customary in the Shire for the host not only to feed and entertain the guests but also to *give* each one a birthday present. This was a problem because Buckley's cabbage crop failed, and he could only afford to invite thirty hobbits to his party.

Buckley's wife wanted him to invite their well-off neighbors, therefore making sure that they will be asked to the best parties over the next year. Buckley's son thought that all the neighbors' and relatives' names should be put in a hat and the first thirty names pulled out should be invited. Buckley's uncle was of the opinion that having a party would be foolish, and it should be cancelled. Buckley's sister reasoned the fair thing to do would be to invite those who really wanted to come. She thought a way to manage this would be to place a numbered sheet of paper by the gate and announce that the first thirty hobbits signing up would be invited.

Buckley listened to all of his family members and considered their views at great length. He knew however, that the final decision would be his and his alone to make.

Economics & Enterpreneurship

Economic Systems of Middle-earth

Buckley's Birthday Bash Dilemma
Solution

DIRECTIONS: Using the situation described on Visual 2 answer the questions below. Use complete sentences.

1. What is Buckley Brandybuck's major scarcity problem?

2. What are some possible problems with the solutions suggested by Buckley's family members?

    1). His wife's suggestion- only to invite the wealthy

    2). His son's suggestion – conduct a lottery

    3). His uncle's suggestion – skip the party

    4). His sister's suggestion – first come/first serve

3. What do you think is the best solution for Buckley's problem? Describe how you think he should allocate the invitations to his party in such a manner as not to suffer too much socially or economically.

© Pieces of Learning

Economics & Enterpreneurship
Galleons, Sickles, and Knuts

"Once Harry had refilled his money bag with gold Galleons, silver Sickles, and bronze Knuts from his vault at Gringotts, he had to exercise a lot of self-control not to spend the whole lot at once."

- J.K. Rowling describing Harry's stay at Diagon Alley
Harry Potter and the Prisoner of Azkaban

Harry Potter and the Prisoner of Azkaban
By J.K. Rowling

STORY SYNOPSIS

Harry is now about to enter his third year at Hogwarts School of Witchcraft and Wizardry. Our young hero has caused a major upset at his Uncle Vernon's house, where he stays in the summer, and finds himself a runaway taking sanctuary in Diagon Alley. He needs to rest, because this year will be one of life changing encounters and discoveries. Harry's encounters include the dreadful dementors, a new Defense Against the Dark Arts professor, Remus Lupin, and his first-hated-then-loved godfather, Sirius Black. (It is Sirius Black who is the prisoner of Azkaban.) The discoveries include facts about his parents, the magic Marauder's Map and the true identity of Ron's rat Scabbers. The story concludes with Harry and Hermione turning back time and saving the day.

CONTENT CONNECTION

Money plays an important part in book three of the Harry Potter series. The story begins with the normally poor Wesley family winning the annual *Daily Prophet* Grand Prize Galleon Draw. This circumstance sets a chain of events into action that includes a trip to Egypt, a jailbreak, and the unveiling of a hidden enemy.

Also important to the plot is the fact that while Harry is a wealthy young man in the Wizarding world, he is totally dependent on his relatives for financial support in the Muggle, or non magical, world. Much to Harry's dismay, while it is possible to convert Muggle money into Galleons, Sickles, and Knuts, it does not work the other way around.

TIME REQUIRED: 40-45 minutes.

© Pieces of Learning

Economics & Enterpreneurship

Galleons, Sickles, and Knuts

OBJECTIVES
- The student will define money as an agreed upon medium of exchange that has specific attributes.
- The student will participate in an exchange activity.
- The student will define, money, barter, and goods and services.
- The student may participate in the extension activity dealing with the development of a unique monetary system.

MATERIALS
- Visual - **Attributes of Money** (p.40)
- Visual - **Exchange Activity** (p. 41)
- Water soluble marker
- Cut out paper coins, Galleons, Sickles, and Knuts (p.42) - enough for each student to get about 6-7 coins
- Cut out **Wizard World Goods and Services** cards (p.43) - enough for each student to get about four cards
- Envelopes - one for each student

PROCEDURE
1. Prepare the visuals, coins, and cards prior to class. The coins and cards can be reproduced on card stock to make them more durable. Each student will need a prepared envelope with about ten items in it. (This activity works well if each student receives about 6 coins and 4 goods and services cards. Do NOT worry about equality in this activity. Like much of life, the envelope each student receives will be "the luck of the draw.")

2. Start the lesson by asking students what money is. (You will probably be told that it is green paper.)

3. Define money as "anything generally accepted in exchange for goods and services."

4. Display the visual **Attributes of Money**. Read the information to the students. Solicit responses in order to fill in the chart. Answers may vary from class to class.

5. Tell the students that now that they have discussed money they will participate in an interactive activity.

6. Display the visual **Exchange Activity** and read it to the class. Ask if there are any questions to check for understanding.

7. Pass out prepared Exchange Activity envelopes to each student. Allow them to take a short time to investigate the contents.

8. Start the activity by saying *"The Exchange Market is Now Open."*

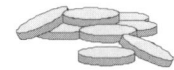

© Pieces of Learning

Economics & Enterpreneurship

Galleons, Sickles, and Knuts

9. Allow about 5-10 minutes for the students to interact.

10. Stop the activity by saying "The Exchange Market is Now Closed."
    Note: Students need to put coins and cards back into the envelopes. The envelopes' contents will now be very different from the start of the activity. If another class is coming in directly after this one don't worry about it. It makes for a more interesting second round!

EVALUATION
Ask the students these questions at the end of the Exchange Activity. There are no predictable answers. However, students tend to enjoy the activity and should come away with the concept that money is "anything generally accepted in exchange for goods and services."

- ❖ Was everyone able to make three exchanges, either by bartering or purchasing the desired item?
- ❖ What was the most popular item, the one in greatest demand? Why do you think this was?
- ❖ What was the least favorite item, the one the most difficult to exchange? Why do you think this was?
- ❖ How many people are happy with the contents in your envelopes? If so, would you consider yourself wealthy?

EXTENSION
Creative students may find that they are interested in designing a currency that could be used in one of their favorite pieces of literature.

Make Your Own "Fantastic" Money
Create a monetary system for one of these fantasylands found in literature.

The Emerald City - *The Wonderful Wizard of Oz*
Narnia – *The Lion, the Witch, and the Wardrobe*
Wonderland – *Through the Looking Glass*
Lilliput – *Gulliver's Travels*
Neverland – *Peter Pan*
The Shire – *The Hobbit*
Dictionopolis and/or Digitopolis – *The Phantom Tollbooth*
Or choose a favorite imaginary land of your own)

> ➢ Design the currency
> ➢ Develop the denominations that will be available
> ➢ Discuss what makes this money durable, valuable, and distinctive

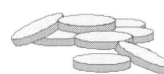

© Pieces of Learning

Economics & Enterpreneurship

Galleons, Sickles, and Knuts

Attributes of Money

Money can be defined as "anything generally accepted in exchange for goods and services." Throughout history and in literature different items have been regarded as money. Complete the table below. Write the answer **YES, NO,** or **UNKNOWN** in the squares if you think the currency listed meets the listed attributes.

Defined – Has a society agreed to use this item as money?
Portable – Can the money be easily used and transported from place to place?
Durable – Is the money strong? Will it last a long time?
Divisible – Can the money be divided into smaller parts or do units exist?
Distinctive – Is the money relatively rare? Would it be difficult to reproduce it?

CURRENCY	Defined	Portable	Durable	Divisible	Distinctive
Buck Skins Native Americans					
Tobacco Early Colonist					
Trading Cards School Yard					
Dollars U.S.A. Currency					
Galleons Magical Realm					

 What did you learn about money from this activity?

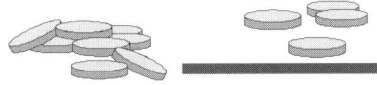

Economics & Enterpreneurship

Galleons, Sickles, and Knuts

Exchange Activity
Introduction

In Harry Potter's Wizarding World three types of coins are used as currency.

Gold Galleons

Silver Sickles (17 Sickles = 1 Galleon)

Bronze Knuts (29 Knuts = 1 Sickle)

There are also different types of goods and services sold in the shops; things such as magic wands and chocolate frogs. This activity will use pretend money and merchandise from Harry's world.

Directions for Exchange Activity

- Each person will receive an envelope containing coins and goods and services cards.
- Upon hearing the words "The Exchange Market is Now Open" each person is to make at least 3 exchanges. This may be done through selling an item for currency or bartering (trading) one item for another.
- The goal is to make the most advantageous exchanges possible.
- Exchanging may continue until it is announced "The Exchange Market is Now Closed."
- Return to your seats and be prepared to discuss the activity.

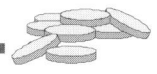

© Pieces of Learning

Economics & Enterpreneurship

Galleons, Sickles, and Knuts

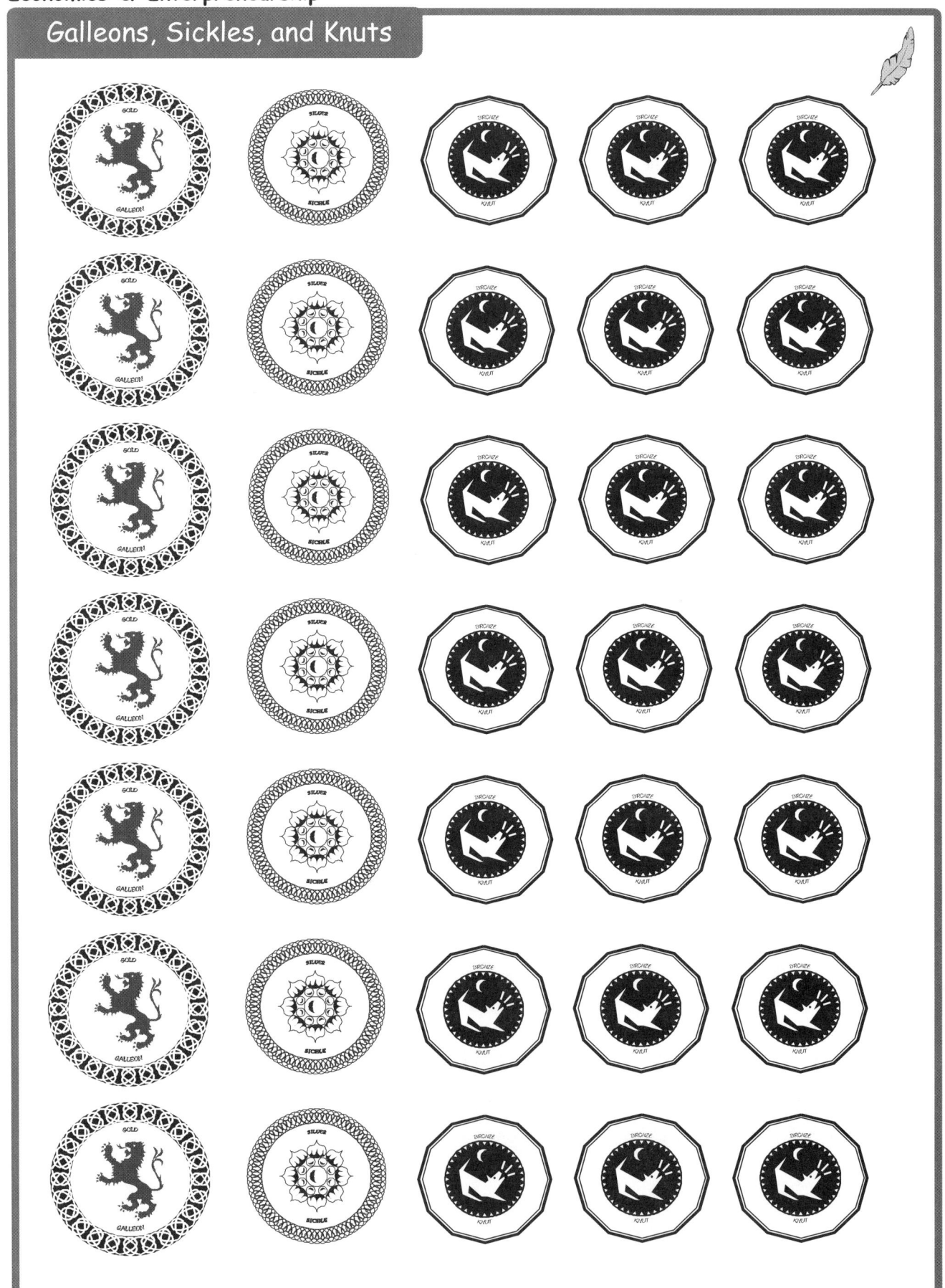

Economics & Enterpreneurship

Galleons, Sickles, and Knuts

Wizard World Goods and Services

Pumpkin Pasty 	A ride on the Hogwarts Express 	A Magic Book that reads to you. 
Magic Broom *The Firebolt* 	Chocolate Frog 	Magic Wand 
Bertie Bott's Every Flavor Beans 	Magic Stick Bombs 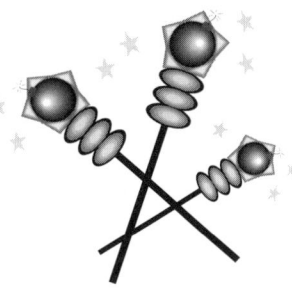	Pet Cat 
Owl Delivery Service 	Caldron for Potions 	Class Magic Map 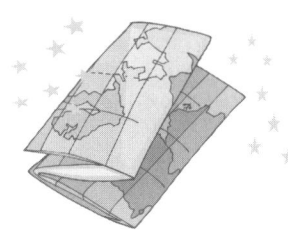

© Pieces of Learning

Economics & Enterpreneurship

Charlie's Chocolates

> *"This is the most important room in the entire factory! All of my most secret new inventions are cooking and simmering in here!"*
>
> — Willy Wonka
> *Charlie and the Chocolate Factory*

Charlie and the Chocolate Factory
By Roald Dahl

STORY SYNOPSIS

Willy Wonka, entrepreneur extraordinaire, is opening his famous chocolate factory for the first time in ten years. Also a marketing mastermind, Mr. Wonka devises a unique promotional plan. He announces that five golden tickets have been placed under the wrappers of his delicious candy bars. The holders of these tickets will be given a personal tour of his mysterious factory.

At the last minute, our hero, young Charlie Bucket, finds the final ticket and joins four other children and their chaperones for an amazing tour of one of the most extraordinary factories in the world. One by one the other winners let personality flaws undermine their chances of winning the respect of the marvelous Mr. Wonka. By the end of the tour, only Charlie and his grandfather remain. Charlie's reward for his honesty is the chocolate factory itself!

CONTENT CONNECTION

Entrepreneurs are defined as people who organize, manage, and assume the risks of a business or enterprise. Mr. Willy Wonka of *Charlie and the Chocolate Factory* fame exhibits all of these characteristics. To add to his entrepreneurial qualities, he is inventive, energetic, and charismatic. He also displays many of the other "intangible" qualities often found in successful entrepreneurs. He is independent, a high achiever, and possesses an indomitable spirit that sets him apart from others.

Poor and lovable Charlie Bucket may not realize it but he, too, is a risk- taker. How else can it be explained that when he found money on the street he used it to buy candy bars instead of food for his hungry family? Students will also become risk takers when they design, name, and promote their own sweet product.

TIME REQUIRED: 40-50 minutes.

© Pieces of Learning

Economics & Enterpreneurship

Charlie's Chocolates

OBJECTIVES
- The student will define and discuss the characteristics of an entrepreneur.
- The student will emulate some of the characteristics of an entrepreneur by designing, naming, and promoting a product.
- The student may participate in the extension activity dealing with famous entrepreneurs and their contributions to society.

MATERIALS
- Visual - **Willy Wonka, Entrepreneur** (p.48)
- Water-soluble marker.
- Activity – **Candy Craze** (p.49) - a copy for each group
- An assortment of candies such as marshmallows, M&M's®, jellybeans, liquorish whips, and peanut butter cups. (This activity is often done after a major holiday when seasonal treats go on sale.)
- Optional – Extension Activity - **Entrepreneurs Extraordinaire** (p.50)

PROCEDURE
1. Explain to the students that after a brief introduction lesson they will be participating in a group hands-on activity. Inform them that excellent behavior is an expectation.

2. Display the Visual **Willy Wonka, Entrepreneur**. Read the definition and ask the students how they would rank the six characteristics. Record their ideas. While entrepreneurs usually rank this list as 1. Competitive 2. Self-confident 3. Risk-taker 4. Energetic 5. Creative and 6. Organized, the list is subjective. If the students are ranking the characteristics of the fictional Willy Wonka, energetic will probably be first.

3. Ask the students the question on the bottom of the visual *Can you think of any other characteristics that might describe a successful entrepreneur?* Write their suggestions under the question on the visual. Possible answers: *Power hungry, leader, strong, desire for wealth, healthy*

4. Explain to the students that they are now going to get an opportunity to be risk-takers. Tell the students that they will be working in groups of three or four members. (They may choose their own groups, use already existing co-operative learning groups, or you may group them.)

5. Distribute copies of the activity **Candy Craze** to each group. (A transparency may be made of the activity for display as the assignment is explained to the students.)

6. Review the activity with the class.

© Pieces of Learning

Economics & Enterpreneurship

Charlie's Chocolates

7. Allow each group to send a representative to the area in which the supply of candy is displayed. Allocate the amount each group may use. This will depend on the supply. It is usually effective if each group is allowed ten items. (They quickly figure out that the marshmallows can be used like glue.)

8. Allocate 15-20 minutes for the groups to complete their prototype. (Give them a five-minute warning.)

9. Encourage the students to share their solutions with the class. Collect the activity sheets when the presentation is complete for grading purposes.

10. Congratulate them on their creativity and ability to work under pressure. Give them a few minutes to clean up.

EVALUATION

While this activity is a creative group activity it is still important that the students know they are accountable for their solution to the challenge. The point system on the bottom works well in evaluating the students' work. If a resource specialist is conducting this lesson, the grades should be shared with the classroom teacher. Note that most of the points are for cooperation and a good work ethic.

- Group Participation 1-40 points
- Use of Materials 1-20 points
- Complete Worksheet 1-20
- Creativeness 1-10 points
- Clean Workstation 1-10 points

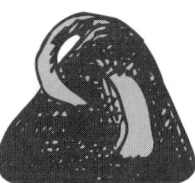

Economics & Enterpreneurship

Charlie's Chocolates

EXTENSION

Entrepreneurs may have certain characteristics in common, but they are as diverse as any other group. Students may wish to study famous entrepreneurs to discover more about what makes them so successful. The activity **Entrepreneurs Extraordinaire** may be introduced to a small group of students as an enrichment activity or to the entire class as an extended assignment that may be monitored by the classroom teacher.

Students may choose to do the research required using reference books and periodicals. However, it may be more appropriate, if one of the contemporary entrepreneurs is chosen, to use the Internet for research.

© Pieces of Learning

Economics & Enterpreneurship

Charlie's Chocolates

Willy Wonka, Entrepreneur

Entrepreneurs are defined as people who organize, manage, and assume the risks of a business or enterprise. Willy Wonka, a very successful businessman in the story *Charlie and the Chocolate Factory* by Roald Dahl had all of these qualities plus many others. Below is a list of characteristics that many entrepreneurs possess. Rank them in order of importance YOU think these characteristics are to becoming a successful entrepreneur. Consider 1 as the most important and 6 as the least important.

___ Competitive

___ Energetic

___ Organized

___ Self-confident

___ Risk-taker

___ Creative

Can you think of any other characteristics that might describe a successful entrepreneur?

Economics & Enterpreneurship

Charlie's Chocolates

Candy Craze

Introduction: You may have heard of Everlasting Gobstoppers® the candy invented by Willy Wonka in the book *Charlie and the Chocolate Factory* by Roald Dahl. The idea of a piece of candy that would last forever, while impossible, is still fun to imagine.

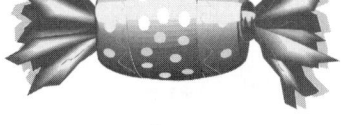

Your Challenge

Using the available "edible" samples as inspiration, create your own new "Candy Craze." Fill in the information concerning your new product below. Be prepared to present your ideas to the class.

Product Name: _____

Five Unique Facts About this Product:

1.
2.
3.
4.
5.

Catchy Slogan or Jingle: _____

_____

Rating Scale:

_____ Group Participation 1-40 points

_____ Use of Materials 1-20 points

_____ Complete Worksheet 1-20

_____ Creativeness 1-10 points

_____ Clean Workstation 1-10 points

© Pieces of Learning

Economics & Enterpreneurship
Charlie's Chocolates

Entrepreneurs Extraordinaire

In the United States the growth of the economy is directly connected to individuals who take risks and start new businesses. These entrepreneurs see a need to introduce a new product, a service, or a technology to consumers.

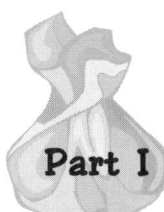

Part I

Choose one of the entrepreneurs below to research. List at list ten interesting facts about this person. (You may also research an entrepreneur of your choosing.)

1. Walt Disney
2. Thomas Alva Edison
3. Henry Ford
4. Benjamin Franklin
5. Bill Gates
6. Isaac Singer
7. Martha Stewart
8. Dave Thomas
9. Eli Whitney
10. Oprah Winfrey

Part II

Answer these questions in your report:
- Was it necessary for this person to overcome any obstacle to achieve his/her goals?
- What product, service, or technology did this person introduce?
- Has society benefited from this person's entrepreneurial spirit?

© Pieces of Learning

History & Civics

The Pockets of Presidents

"In the right waistcoat pocket we found a prodigious bundle of white thin substances, folded one over another, about the bigness of three men. They were tied with strong cable and marked with black figures that we think to be writing. Every letter is almost half as the palm of our hands."

- From a report to the Lilliputian Emperor Concerning the Diary in Gulliver's pocket.

Gulliver's Travels
By Jonathan Swift

STORY SYNOPSIS

Irishman Jonathan Swift originally wrote his book, *Gulliver's Travels*, as a satire. The tale describes the adventures of 18th century Englishman Doctor Lemuel Gulliver as he visits four very different imaginary countries. Gulliver first finds himself washed ashore on the land of Lilliput. Here he is a giant, towering over the politically motivated population. After many adventures, and being charged with treason, he escapes and is rescued by an English ship. He is not home long when he returns to sea and discovers himself in Brobdingnag, the land of giants. Here he ponders moral issues while being caged and displayed as an oddity. He returns home to his family only to leave again. Pirates attack this ship. Gulliver escapes and discovers a new unusual country. It is the floating cloud of Balnibarbi. The Laputans who live here value "intellectualism" and the principles of math, music, and science over everything else. Gulliver's last trip finds him visiting the Houyhnhnms and the Yahoos, the first being intelligent horses and the second vulgar beasts. Here he suffers a major change in life style and upon returning home is a much-changed man.

CONTENT CONNECTION

A piece of classic literature, *Gulliver's Travels* was written as an adult satire over 250 years ago. Because of the fantastic settings and silly characters, young people find the story exciting. (Most students and teachers will need a contemporary version to understand the dated language.) A great deal of the humor in the story of Gulliver's adventurers stem from communication problems and cultural misunderstandings. This lesson encourages students to use prior knowledge to interpret items that might have been found in the "Pockets of Presidents" much the same way the objects found in Gulliver's pockets were used to deduce things about him.

TIME REQUIRED: 25-30 minutes.

History & Civics

The Pockets of Presidents

OBJECTIVES
- The student will participate in a group activity accessing prior knowledge of American Presidents.
- The student will discover how an individual's possessions reveal information concerning the person's identity.
- The student will be introduced to the definition for satire.
- The student may participate in the extension activity dealing with the artifacts and possessions that might be found in other famous people's pockets.

MATERIALS
- Visual - **Informative Inventory: What the Lilliputians found in Gulliver's Pockets** (p.54)
- Visual - **Which Presidents' Pocket? Item Inventory** (p.55)
- Activity - **Informative Inventory of Presidents' Pockets** (p.56)
- Pens and pencils
- Water soluble pen
- Optional – *Gulliver's Travels* books and United States Presidents reference books.

PROCEDURE
1. Prepare the visual and worksheets ahead of class.

2. Ask the students if they have ever heard of the classic book *Gulliver's Travels* by Jonathan Swift. Explain that it was written many years ago as a satire. Explain that **satire** is writing that makes fun of people's faults and weaknesses. **Satire** is often used to raise questions and concerns about current fads, popular culture, or politics.

3. Display Visual - **Informative Inventory: What the Lilliputians found in Gulliver's Pockets**. Tell the students that when Gulliver found himself in the land of the little people of Lilliput they demanded to look in his pockets to see if he had anything of danger in them. Read the list with the students. Ask them to brainstorm ideas concerning Gulliver. Record and discuss these ideas on the visual. [Possible responses: *He knew how to shoot a gun. He used snuff. He was educated because he could write. He was a full-grown man because he needed a razor to shave. He was wealthy- He had a watch and money. He was able to defend himself. He must have had really big pockets! He was not bald. He might have had a cold or have been sick and needed the handkerchief. He lived long ago when powder was needed for pistols.*]

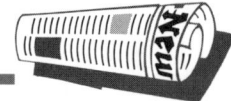

© Pieces of Learning

History & Civics

The Pockets of Presidents

4. Display the Visual - **Which President's Pocket? Item Inventory.** Read the list of items to the class. Ask the students to use clues to identify the president who may have had these items in his possession. [They should be able to identify Franklin Delano Roosevelt.]

5. Explain to the students that they will be asked to use the clues to identify four more presidents. Pass out the activity sheets. Students may work in groups or independently. (This may also be done as a whole class activity.)

6. Allow students to use reference materials if they need help with identifying the correct president.

7. Check the answers as a group.

8. Conclude the activity by asking the students if they would be able to be identified by the objects they carry in their pockets!

EVALUATION

Answers to Activity – **Informative Inventory of Presidents' Pockets**
1. John Fitzgerald Kennedy, 35th President
2. George Washington, 1st President
3. Theodore Roosevelt, 26th President
4. Thomas Jefferson, 3rd President

EXTENSION
There are many ways this lesson can be extended.

➢ Students are assigned or choose a historical figure or literary character. They are to collect actual items that would represent artifacts that might be found in these people's pockets, purses, saddlebags, or briefcases. They are to present these items to class to see if they are able to reveal the identity of the chosen character.

➢ The classroom teacher may wish to use this activity for a review, creating hypothetical pocket contents for historical characters the students are studying.

➢ The students may develop a list of items for historical figures or literary characters as a part of a game to challenge other students as to their knowledge.

© Pieces of Learning
The Pockets of Presidents
53

History & Civics

The Pockets of Presidents

Informative Inventory
What the Lilliputians found in Gulliver's Pockets

Comb
Copper and Silver Coins
Diary
Handkerchief
Knife
Pistols
Pouch of Powder and Bullets
Purse Holding Nine Gold Pieces
Razor
Saber
Snuff Box
Watch

What might this list tell you about Gulliver's skills, habits, personality traits, and professional occupation? Create a list of ten ideas that can be inferred from the items recorded above.

1.
2.
3.
4.
5.
6.
7.
8.
9.
10.

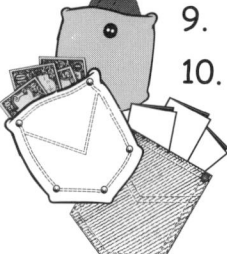

History & Civics

The Pockets of Presidents

Which Presidents' Pocket?
Item Inventory

- Notes of ideas for his radio "Fireside Chats"
- A pack of cigarettes and a cigarette holder
- A letter from England written by his wife Eleanor, who was well known to act as his "eyes and legs"
- A pair of eyeglasses
- A newspaper article about the Dust Bowl
- A lapel button promoting the Civilian Conservation Corps

Which United States President might carry these items in his pockets?

What makes you think so?

Answer: _____

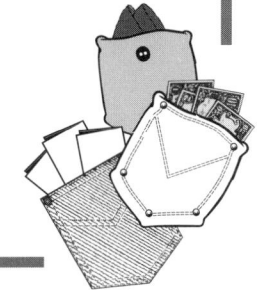

© Pieces of Learning

55

History & Civics

The Pockets of Presidents

Informative Inventory Of
Presidents' Pockets

Can you guess what United States President might have the following items in his pocket? Write your answer on the appropriate line.

-1-
- A Military medal – the Purple Heart
- Candy for his small daughter and son
- A brochure explaining the new Peace Core program
- A note to his wife "Jackie"
- A small notebook with questions and concerns about Cuba

President _____

-2-
- A letter to his wife at Mount Vernon
- An extra set of springs for his false teeth
- A notebook about farming
- An apple for his horse
- A small cherry tart
- A tin of powder for his white wig

President _____

-3-
- A pair of wire-rimmed eye glasses
- A small "teddy bear"
- A book about boxing
- A pair of driving gloves
- A big stick
- A note to write a letter to the Wright Brothers

President _____

-4-
- A quill pen and parchment
- A letter from Meriwether Lewis
- A key to the front door of Monticello
- Small architectural sketches for the University of Virginia
- A packet of tomato seeds
- An invitation to a violin recital

President _____

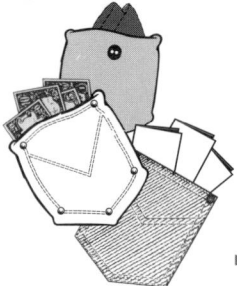

History & Civics

Captain Cook & Captain Hook: Fact or Fiction?

*"Avast, belay, when I appear,
By fear they're overtook;
Nought's left upon your bones when you
Have shaken claws with Hook."*

- Pirate Chant
Peter Pan

Peter Pan
By J.M. Barrie

STORY SYNOPSIS

Peter Pan, written by Sir James Matthew Barrie, was originally written as a play in 1904. This classic tale starts in the very conventional home of the Darling family. While the parents are away the children, Wendy, John, and Michael are visited by the forever-young Peter Pan and his loyal fairy friend, Tinker Bell. Peter, who can fly, teaches the children to fly, too. He persuades them to follow him to Neverland, a magical place inhabited by mermaids, fairies, and pirates. Also living here are his followers, the Lost Boys. (These boys have lived in Neverland since falling out of their carriages as babies.) The Darling children have many adventures with Peter who, while immature and totally self-absorbed, is charismatic and a born leader. Peter's chief nemesis is the extremely evil Captain James Hook. This pirate captain has lost his right hand thanks to Peter and has vowed his revenge. In the end it is Captain Hook who is defeated. Mermaids, Indians, and the Never Bird all play a part in the story of a boy who never wants to be a man and a young girl who is not afraid to grow up.

CONTENT CONNECTION

The story of *Peter Pan*, now considered a classic, reflects the times in which it was written. The theme of the Victorian family, especially the importance of motherhood, is woven throughout. Also, England's class system is mirrored in Captain Hook and his interaction with his crew. Even though *Peter Pan* is representative of a specific time and place, Barrie's inventive story of a boy who refuses to grow up has proven to be universal and timeless.

TIME REQUIRED: 25-30 minutes.

History & Civics

Captain Cook & Captain Hook: Fact or Fiction?

OBJECTIVES
- The student will participate in an activity identifying historical and literary figures.
- The student will complete a worksheet concerning fact and fiction.
- The student may participate in the extension activity dealing with the creation of business cards for historical and/or literary figures.

MATERIALS
- Visual - **Captain Cook & Captain Hook: Fact or Fiction?** (p.61)
- Activity Sheet - **Captain Cook & Captain Hook: Fact or Fiction?** (p.62) - one for each student or group
- Water soluble marker
- Pens and/or pencils

PROCEDURE
1. Prepare materials prior to class.

2. Start class by asking the students if they can tell you the difference between fact and fiction. (A fact is something that can be verified to be true; fiction is something that has been created from someone's imagination.)

3. Display the visual **Captain Cook & Captain Hook: Fact or Fiction?** Read the introduction for the class. Solicit answers for the five characters listed.

    Billy the Kid – FACT Henry McCarty, alias Kid Antrim, alias William H. Bonney, was a notorious outlaw who was killed in 1881 by lawman Pat Garrett.

    Tom Sawyer – FICTION He is the mischievous main character in Mark Twain's *The Adventures of Tom Sawyer*.

    Annie Oakley – FACT Phoebe Anne Oakley Mozee was a sharp shooter in Buffalo Bill's Wild West Show.

    Ebenezer Scrooge FICTION He is a miserly character from Charles Dickens's *A Christmas Carol*.

    David Copperfield FACT and FICTION (Trick Question!) Main character in a book by Charles Dickens of the same name OR a current popular magician.

4. Distribute activity sheet **Captain Cook & Captain Hook: Fact or Fiction?** Students may work independently or in groups.

5. Read the directions to the class. Allow about ten minutes to complete the assignment.

6. Check as a group. (See Evaluation)

© Pieces of Learning

History & Civics

Captain Cook & Captain Hook: Fact or Fiction?

EVALUATION

Check the students' work with the answers below. Students are encouraged to contribute more information about the people on the list. Award them bonus points for additional information. (Note - this is a good introductory lesson for a biography unit.)

1. **Johnny Appleseed**   FACT John Chapman was Massachusetts man who planted apple seeds all over Ohio and Indiana.

2. **Marco Polo**   FACT He was an Italian explorer who was one of the first Europeans to visit China.

3. **Sherlock Holmes**   FICTION He was a clever detective in mystery stories by Sir Arthur Conan Doyle.

4. **Calamity Jane**   FACT   Martha Jane Canary was a Montana tomboy who grew up to ride for the Pony Express.

5. **Kit Carson**   FACT   Christopher Carson was an Indian Agent, Scout, and Civil War Officer.

6. **Ichabod Crane**   FICTION   The skinny schoolteacher is the main character in Washington Irving's *The Legend of Sleepy Hollow*.

7. **Lizzie Borden**   FACT   Did she kill her parents with an ax in Massachusetts in 1892? No one knows for sure.

8. **King Arthur**   FICTION   He is the legendary king of Camelot.

9. **Michaelangelo**   FACT   He was a famous Renaissance artist.

10. **Rip Van Winkle**   FICTION He was the main character in a story by Washington Irving about a man who went to sleep for 20 years in the Catskill Mountains.

© Pieces of Learning

History & Civics

Captain Cook & Captain Hook: Fact or Fiction?

EXTENSION

Creative Business Cards

Many professional people carry business cards. These small cards serve as a quick method to give interested people and potential clients information in case contact needs to be made in the future. Might Captain Hook's 21st century business card look like this?

Pirating, Plundering, Prowling and Pillaging

Captain James Hook
Pirate Ship   1-800 – PIECES of GOLD
Neverland
                 jhook@neverland.gov

Create a business for one of the historical figures or fictional literary characters listed below. (You may also choose one of your own.) Your card should include name, business, address, and contact information. Slogans, logos, mottos, etc. may also be incorporated into your business card design.

Historic

Julius Caesar
George Washington Carver
Thomas Jefferson
Benedict Arnold

Fictional

Superman
Snow White
Sherlock Holmes
Robinson Crusoe

© Pieces of Learning

History & Civics

Captain Cook & Captain Hook: Fact or Fiction?

Captain Cook & Captain Hook: Fact or Fiction?

It is true that some historical figures have had such extraordinary lives that they seem legendary. It is also true that some literary characters have been so brilliantly written they seem to have been a part of our history.

For example:
James Cook was an English sea captain whose explorations lead him to Australia, the Antarctic Circle, and the Pacific Islands.

James Hook was an English sea captain, with a missing right hand, who, with his crew of cutthroat pirates, terrorized Neverland.

James Cook, 18th Century explorer, is **factual** or **real**.

James Hook, pirate captain in J.M. Barrie's story, *Peter Pan* is **fictional** or **make believe**.

Which of the following do you think are factual? Which do you think are fictional?

Billy the Kid
Tom Sawyer
Annie Oakley
Ebenezer Scrooge
David Copperfield

© Pieces of Learning

History & Civics

Captain Cook & Captain Hook: Fact or Fiction?

Captain Cook & Captain Hook: Fact or Fiction?

Directions: Do the names listed below belong to a famous figure in history, like Captain Cook, or are they the product of a wonderful writer's imagination, like Captain Hook? Circle your choice, fact or fiction. (An extra point will be rewarded if an interesting fact about the name is written beside the name.)

1. **Johnny Appleseed**   FACT or FICTION
2. **Marco Polo**   FACT or FICTION
3. **Sherlock Holmes**   FACT or FICTION
4. **Calamity Jane**   FACT or FICTION
5. **Kit Carson**   FACT or FICTION
6. **Ichabod Crane**   FACT or FICTION
7. **Lizzie Borden**   FACT or FICTION
8. **King Arthur**   FACT or FICTION
9. **Michaelangelo**   FACT or FICTION
10. **Rip Van Winkle**   FACT or FICTION

Extra, Extra Credit - Can you think of any characters that might fool people that you could add to this list?

62   © Pieces of Learning

History & Civics

Mudbloods, Muggles, and Magic: Prejudices in Potter's World

"Sirius did not hate Kreacher," said Dumbledore. "He regarded him as a servant unworthy of much interest or notice. Indifference and neglect often do much more damage than outright dislike... The fountain we destroyed tonight told a lie. We wizards have mistreated and abused our fellows for too long, and we are now reaping our reward."

- Headmaster Albus Dumbledore
Harry Potter and the Order of the Phoenix

Harry Potter and the Order of the Phoenix
By J.K. Rowling

STORY SYNOPSIS

Harry Potter, now fifteen and in his fifth year a Hogwarts School of Witchcraft and Wizardry, has become a true teenager. His emotional turmoil is understandable. He has had to spend a good deal of the summer with his loathsome relatives, and the communication he does have with his friends leaves a great deal to be desired. He soon discovers that his ordeals of the year before, revealing the return of the evil Lord Voldermort, have sent a powerful chain of events into action. A new "bully" Defense Against the Dark Arts teacher, isolation from adult supporters, recurring nightmares, and the shocking death of a father figure make this school year Harry's most traumatic to date.

CONTENT CONNECTION

The reoccurring themes of racial prejudice and bullying behavior, evident in all of the Harry Potter books, have come to a climax in the fifth book of the series, *Harry Potter and the Order of the Phoenix*. Harry's cousin, Dudley Dursley, has turned into a real thug, terrorizing all of the smaller children in the neighborhood. Draco Malfoy and his cronies still abuse any student at the school who they consider a "Mudblood," someone not born into a Wizarding family. Hermione Granger is still fuming over the slave-like treatment of house elves. The most blatantly prejudiced character is Dolores Umbridge, a power hungry and narrow-minded member of the Ministry of Magic, turned teacher, at Hogwarts. Her hatred of any creature she considers a half-breed turns out to be her undoing. She is unable to see past her bigotry when dealing with the centaurs, themselves not known as fair-minded pacifists.

TIME REQUIRED: 30- 40 minutes.

History & Civics

Mudbloods, Muggles, and Magic: Prejudices in Potter's World

OBJECTIVES
- The student will be introduced to the concept of prejudice as a theme in literature.
- The student will participate in an activity giving them the opportunity to apply various skills.
- The student will construct an Activity Cube.
- The student may participate in the extension activity dealing with various literary works dealing with the consequences of prejudicial behavior.

MATERIALS
- Visual - **Mudbloods, Muggles, and Magic: Prejudices in Potter's World** (p.66)
- Copies of **Activity Cube** (p.67) - one for each student or group
- Water-soluble marker
- Scissors, tape and/or glue, paper, pencils and markers
- Copies of news magazines and newspapers for student use
- Dictionaries
- Several Fairy Tale and Folk Tale Anthologies

PROCEDURE
1. Prepare for the lesson by duplicating the activity sheets, creating the visual, and collecting materials and reference books for student use.

2. Introduce the lesson by displaying and reading the visual **Mudbloods, Muggles, and Magic: Prejudices in Potter's World.**

3. Generate a list of prejudices and bullies, and record them on the transparency using examples from the students. Examples of **prejudices** could be global and include, race, religion, physical appearance, intellect, heritage, wealth, etc. Or students may generate a more specific list with examples from history such as the persecution of the Jews in Nazi Germany and slavery in Colonial America. Specific titles in literature may include *Pride and Prejudice* by Jane Austin and Lois Lowery's *The Giver*. Examples of bullies could include Bugs Meany from the *Encyclopedia Brown Series* by Donald Sobol and Jana, the White Witch from *The Lion the Witch and the Wardrobe* by C.S. Lewis. Historical bullies could include Hitler, Stalin, Senator Joseph McCarthy, etc. (Note: Be very careful to limit references to bullies to those in literature and history. No school or community members are to be placed on the list!)

4. Divide the students into groups. (Individual students may also do this activity.)

5. Give each group an **Activity Cube** sheet, scissors and glue or tape and have them cut out the pattern and construct the cube. (To save time, this may be done ahead of time, but the students enjoy the construction process.)

© Pieces of Learning

History & Civics

Mudbloods, Muggles, and Magic: Prejudices in Potter's World

6. Instruct the students that once the cube is complete, they are to roll it. Upon rolling, they are to complete the task that is face up. You may either stretch or condense the lesson depending on the ability of the students and the time available for the lesson. Allowing the students to complete three different activities is a good target.

7. Allow the groups to share one of their completed activities with the class.

EVALUATION

This lesson is an excellent tie-in to Social Studies Units dealing with U.S. Slavery, the Holocaust, the Cold War, etc. The student's pre-knowledge of history and literature will dictate the direction the lesson takes.

Collaboration with the classroom teacher will be necessary for the evaluation of student learning.

EXTENSION

Students often see themselves as victims of circumstances beyond their control. Encourage them to investigate their feelings by reading books about young people who overcame bullying and prejudice. The list below is a small sample of titles dealing with these themes.

Among the Hidden by Margaret Peterson Haddix
Holes by Louis Sachar
Loser by Jerry Spinelli
Maniac Magee by Jerry Spinelli
Mississippi Bridge by Mildred D. Taylor
Number the Stars by Lois Lowery
Roll of Thunder, Hear My Cry by Mildred Taylor
The Star Fisher by Laurence Yep
View from Saturday by E.L. Koningsburg
The Watsons Go to Birmingham - 1963 by Christopher Curtis

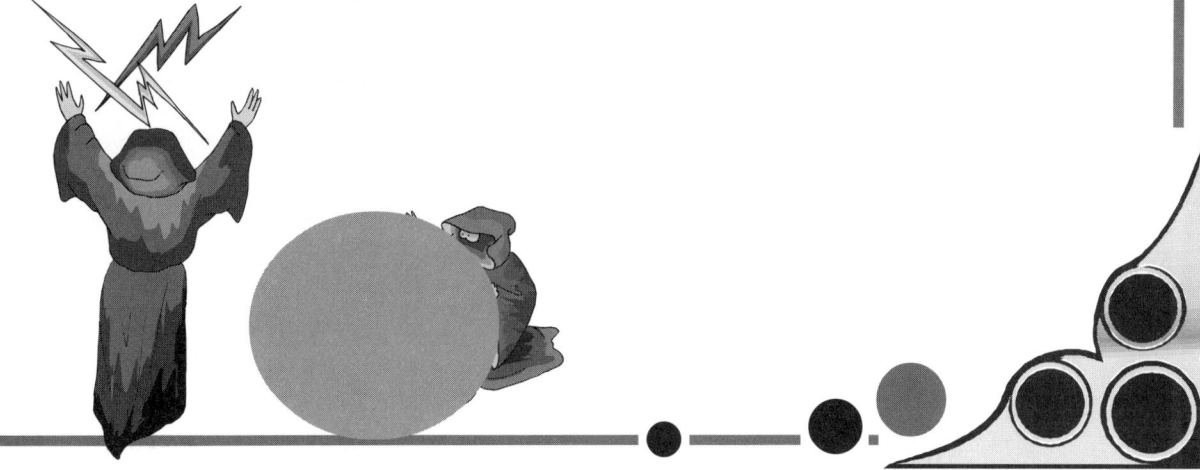

© Pieces of Learning

History & Civics

Mudbloods, Muggles, and Magic: Prejudices in Potter's World

Mudbloods, Muggles, and Magic: Prejudices in Potter's World

Throughout history individuals and groups have persecuted other people. Their intolerance and mistreatment of others may be due to fear, misunderstandings, or just plain meanness and ignorance. We call this behavior **prejudice.** Many examples of prejudicial behavior can be found in J.K. Rowling's fantasy book *Harry Potter and the Order of the Phoenix*. For example, one group of wizards persecutes another because they have Muggle, or non-magical, parents. The centaurs disown one of the herd's members because he befriends humans. And members of Ministry of Magic try to discredit Harry because they do not want to believe that Lord Voldermort has returned.

An individual who picks on others because of prejudice is often called a "bully." In Harry Potter's world, Dudley Dursley, Draco Malfoy, and Professor Umbridge would be excellent examples of bullies.

Using examples from Literature and/or History create a list of ten prejudices that one group may have had against another.

1.   6.
2.   7.
3.   8.
4.   9.
5.   10.

Using examples from Literature and/or History create a list of ten bullies.

1.   6.
2.   7.
3.   8.
4.   9.
5.   10.

66   © Pieces of Learning

History & Civics

Mudbloods, Muggles, and Magic: Prejudices in Potter's World

Activity Cube

Using a dictionary define the words **prejudice**, **intolerance**, and **bully**.

List three fairy tales that include a form of prejudice in the story's plot. (Be ready to defend your choices.)

List ten characteristics of a bully.

Complete a poem with the first line "A bully in school does not need to rule."

Design a poster that would promote **equal** and **fair** treatment for all student and staff members in your school.

Find an example of a news story in a current periodical concerning a form of prejudice. Cut it out, and be prepared to share it with the class.

Cut out the pattern. Fold into a cube. Use the dotted-line flaps and tape to secure the sides.

© Pieces of Learning

67

History & Civics

Pullman's Propaganda: The Power of the Press

"Don't trust your senses. The truth is not what you see. It's what you don't."

Dr. Septimus Prosser, Philosopher
As quoted in the *Daily Scourge*,
in *I Was A Rat!*

I Was A Rat!
By Philip Pullman

STORY SYNOPSIS

When a little boy dressed in a dirty page's uniform arrives at the door of Old Bob and Joan, they don't know what to think. To complicate matters the boy, who they name Roger, insists that he is a rat. The kind couple has always wanted a child and does their best to try to get help from the bureaucracy in finding Roger's family. Periodically there will be a break in the narrative and the reader will be treated to a page from *The Daily Scourge*, a tabloid that is covering the exciting events that revolve around the upcoming marriage of the local prince and the mysterious discovery of a "rat boy."

CONTENT CONNECTION

In Pullman's humorous children's story, *I Was A Rat!*, the print media has the amazing power to influence the opinions of the general public...not unlike the media of today. Throughout the tale the reader is made aware of facts that are being manipulated, misunderstood, and deliberately misreported by the reporters of *The Daily Scourge*. The only motive behind this "yellow press" reporting is the selling of more papers and, therefore, making a greater profit. The methods used by the reporters in *The Daily Scourge* cover many of the better known propaganda techniques. By studying these examples students will be able to identify propaganda and become more news savvy citizens.

TIME REQUIRED: 25-30 minutes.

OBJECTIVES
- The student will be introduced to the terms propaganda, bandwagon, card stacking, glittering generalities, name calling, snob appeal, and testimonials.
- The student will complete a chart using supplied information.
- The student may participate in the extension activity dealing with using propaganda techniques in the creation of an advertisement supporting or degrading a specific subject.

History & Civics

Pullman's Propaganda: The Power of the Press

MATERIALS
- Visual - **Propaganda Power** (p.71)
- Activity - **Rats!** (p.72) - copies for each student or group
- Optional – Newspaper and magazine ads using propaganda techniques
- Optional – A copy of *I Was A Rat!* by Philip Pullman

PROCEDURE

1. Prepare the visual and activity sheets prior to class.

2. Introduce the lesson to the students by telling them that we are being constantly bombarded with messages concerning current events, commercial products, entertainment choices, and many other things every day. Ask them to volunteer the methods that are used to give us these messages. (Possible answers: *television, radio, newspapers, magazines, computer "spam," posters, junk mail*)

3. Display the visual **Propaganda Power**. Explain that all of the examples for the propaganda techniques were taken from the book *I Was A Rat!* by Philip Pullman. Read the visual to the students, soliciting comments and other examples as you do so.

4. Explain that they are going to be completing a chart dealing with the different propaganda techniques that have just been discussed. The intention of these statements is to make rats appear to be wonderful, desirable creatures.

5. Distribute **Rats!** Students may work individually or in groups. Note: Keep the visual displayed for students to use as a reference as they complete the chart.

6. Read the directions and the first technique on the activity sheet to the students. Assure them that their answers may vary. Allow ten to fifteen minutes to complete the activity.

7. Check for understanding as a group.

© Pieces of Learning

69

History & Civics

Pullman's Propaganda: The Power of the Press

EVALUATION
Students' answers should be similar to the ones on the completed chart. Discuss their ideas as you review their work, giving them credit for completing the activity.

Statement	Propaganda Technique	Explanation for Choice
Rats are wonderful creatures; they make great pets, take up very little space, and are extremely easy to feed.	Name Calling	Loaded words like wonderful, great, and extremely were used to give a positive impression about rats.
Beautiful, intelligent, and well-traveled people find that rats make them very happy and popular.	Snob Appeal	This statement makes you feel that to be smart and attractive you had better like rats.
I, Dr. R. O. Dent, feel that the rat is a most superior mammal. My wife Minnie, the famous actress, is a supporter of the R.A.T. foundation.	Testimonials	Dr. Dent and his movie star wife might be important people and support the R.A.T. foundation, but why?
All of your friends have gone to the pet store and bought a superior rat. You should, too. They are terrific!	Bandwagon	The statement reflects the fact that everyone is supporting the idea that Rats are Terrific.
Rats are terrific! They visit lonely people at night and keep the garbage problem under control. The sun shines brighter and the moon glows longer because of the rat.	Glittering Generalities	Statements about the sun, moon, and the kindness of rats are all misleading.
	Card Stacking	The rat is shown to be Santa. Santa brings gifts and is loved by everyone. This shows the rodent to be a giving, jolly creature.

EXTENSION
Have students create a propaganda message. These can be very humorous and are fun to share with the class.

Directions: Create an advertisement supporting one of the following:

Garbage Dumps, The Bubonic Plague, Earthquakes, Tight Fitting Shoes, or something of your choice.
This may be in the form of a newspaper, magazine ad, TV, or radio announcement. Be prepared to share your creation with the class.

History & Civics

Pullman's Propaganda: The Power of the Press

Propaganda Power

Propaganda - the distribution of ideas, information, or hearsay for the intention of assisting or harming an organization or a person.

Propaganda Techniques

Bandwagon - Everyone agrees or is doing something in support of a person or cause. *[EXAMPLE: There was widespread fury today that some so-called scientist will testify on behalf of the rat-monster at the tribunal tomorrow.]*

Card Stacking – Favoritism is shown by using larger print, nicer pictures, or only one side of a circumstance.
EXAMPLE:

> **Your vote**
> Fill in the coupon and send it to us.
>
> Should the evil monster be destroyed?
>
> ☐ **YES**   ☐ no

Glittering Generalities - Broad statements and slogans that sound good but have little substance are made in support of an idea or person. *[EXAMPLE: There is no corner of the world so dark that a little ray of magic from the Princess's heart can't light it up.]*

Name Calling - Using loaded words that will produce strong negative or positive feelings. *[EXAMPLE: This half-human, half rodent, altogether abdominal creature discovered living in the filth of the sewers will demonstrate his loathsome and unnatural appetite by eating anything put before him by the public.]*

Snob Appeal - The "best" people support an idea or product. *[EXAMPLE: We have the finest designers and craftspeople in the world - and here is a chance to show what they can really do.]*

Testimonials - Famous or important people support an idea or product. *[EXAMPLE: Experts believe that the monster is the first of a new breed.]*

History & Civics

Pullman's Propaganda: The Power of the Press

RATS!

The R.A.T. (Rats are Terrific) Society has gone all out to promote rodents in a positive way. They are using propaganda techniques to their advantage. On the chart below a statement, propaganda technique, or explanation has been provided. The missing two parts need to be filled in. This chart must be completed so that we can see just what this "ratty" society is up to!

Statement	Propaganda Technique	Explanation for Choice
Rats are wonderful creatures; they make great pets, take up very little space, and are extremely easy to feed.	Name Calling	Loaded words like wonderful, great, and extremely were used to give a positive impression about rats.
	Snob Appeal	
I, Dr. R. O. Dent, feel that the rat is a most superior mammal. My wife Minnie, the famous actress, is a supporter of the R.A.T. foundation.		
		The statement reflects the fact that everyone is supporting the idea that Rats are Terrific.
	Glittering Generalities	

72 © Pieces of Learning

History & Civics

Faun's Flag and Beaver's Banner

"A wonderful pavilion it was-and especially now when the light of the setting sun fell upon it-with sides of what looked like yellow silk and cords of crimson and tent-pegs of ivory; and high above it on a pole a banner which bore a red rampant lion fluttering in the breeze which was blowing in their faces from the far-off sea."

- Description of area around the Stone Table
The Lion, the Witch and the Wardrobe

The Lion, the Witch and the Wardrobe
By C.S. Lewis

STORY SYNOPSIS
Peter, Susan, Edmund, and Lucy, brothers and sisters, stumble into a magical land after they have been sent to the relative safety of the countryside during the bombings of London in World War II. They are at the country estate of Professor Digory Kirke when they accidentally enter an old wardrobe and find the entryway into the kingdom of Narnia. Here they discover fauns, centaurs, dryads, unicorns, talking beavers, and many other unusual creatures suffering under a spell cast by the evil White Witch. This cold and calculating villain has created a country where it is always winter, but never Christmas. They also meet the brave and wise lion, Aslan, who is working to defeat the White Witch and return Narnia to peace and prosperity. The children prove their bravery in the battle and become Kings and Queens of Narnia. Eventually they return to England through the wardrobe and discover that the professor believes the tale of their adventures in Narnia and foreshadows that they will someday return there.

CONTENT CONNECTION
The lion Aslan leads the different creatures of Narnia into battle under his banner of a red rampant lion. He unifies the land and defeats the evil White Witch. Flag symbolism and national unity appear to be "alive and well" in the land of Narnia.

TIME REQUIRED: 30 - 35 minutes.

OBJECTIVES
- The student will discuss the historical significance of symbols and flags.
- The student will design and create a flag or banner.
- The student may participate in the extension activity designing a global flag.

© Pieces of Learning

History & Civics

Faun's Flag and Beaver's Banner

MATERIALS
- Visuals - **Flag Facts** (p.76) and **Faun's Flag and Beaver's Banner** (p.77)
- Activity sheet - **Faun's Flag and Beaver's Banner** (p.78)
- Optional - Extension Visual - **World Flag** (p.75)
- Markers and colored pencils

PROCEDURE
1. Prepare visuals, activities, and collect materials prior to class.

2. Tell the students that today's lesson will be about flags and the symbolism displayed on them.

3. Display visual **Flag Facts** and read the information to the students. Ask them if they know anything else about flags and flag symbolism. Discuss their comments.

4. Display visual **Faun's Flag and Beaver's Banner**. Read it to the students.

5. Distribute the activity **Faun's Flag and Beaver's Banner** and colored pencils and/or markers. Read the directions to the students. Tell students that the symbols listed are suggestions and that they may use other appropriate ones if they choose. Allow fifteen minutes for the completion of the flag design. (Students may work independently or in groups.) Note: *The teacher may wish to create the list of the people, places, or organizations from which the students may choose to correspond to a specific unit of study.*

6. Ask for volunteers to share their designs with the class.

EVALUATION
Students get full credit for a completed flag or banner that has at least three symbols displayed on it. Students' work may be displayed on bulletin boards

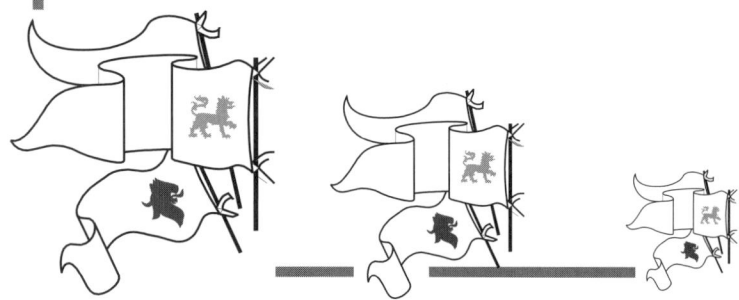

© Pieces of Learning

History & Civics

Faun's Flag and Beaver's Banner

EXTENSION

World Flag

It is the year 2200. The planet Earth has become united and is now a part of an intergalactic organization. Design a flag for either the planet or the organization.

© Pieces of Learning

75

History & Civics

Faun's Flag and Beaver's Banner

Flag Facts

A flag is a piece of cloth with a distinctive design to show nationality, military rank, official office, civic organizations, etc.

Flags were probably first used by the Ancient Egyptians. They were symbols attached to poles. The Chinese were the first to use cloth flags.

During the Middles Ages flags played an important part in the Feudal System.

National flags first came into use in the 18th century. A nation's flag represents a country's government, citizens, heritage, and principles.

    The flag of the United States is the most often modified flag in the world. The thirteen stripes stand for the thirteen original colonies. The fifty stars represent the current number of states.

    The last star was added in 1960 when Hawaii became a state. The colors of the "stars and stripes" also have significance. Red symbolizes strength and courage; white represents innocence and purity; blue stands for vigilance and justice.

 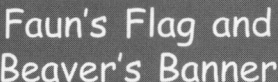

Faun's Flag and Beaver's Banner

Mr. Tumnus, a faun in the land of Narnia, may have designed a flag for himself with a stag and a flute on it. The stag would represent wishful thinking. Mr. Tumnus tells Lucy that if you catch a white stag he will grant your wishes. Mr. Tumnus, like all fauns, is a lover of music, and plays the flute well.

The Beavers, lovers of trees and excellent with a needle and thread, might have designed a banner like this. (Banners are similar to flags but are more often used for decoration and pageantry.)

History & Civics

Faun's Flag and Beaver's Banner

Faun's Flag and Beaver's Banner

Directions – Using the patterns below, design a flag or a banner for a specific person, place or organization, either historic or fictional. Your design should contain three symbols that represent the subject you have chosen. Be prepared to explain your choice of symbols and colors to the class.

Some Symbols and Meanings

Animals
Lion – Courage
Bear – Strength
Bull – Valor
Centaur – Scholarship
Dove – Peace
Dragon – Protection
Eagle – Noble
Hawk – Restless
Horse – Prepared
Peacock – Watchfulness
Serpent – Wise
Stag – Fortitude
Unicorn – Bravery

Objects
Castle – Safety
Holly – Truth
Horseshoe – Good Luck
Lightning Bolt – Power
Oak Tree – Strength
Rainbow – Good following Bad
Rock – Protection
Sword – Justice
Vine – Strong Friendship
Wheel – Wealth

Colors
Black – Grief
Blue – Loyalty
Gold – Generosity
Green – Hope and Love
Orange – Splendor
Purple – Royalty
Red – Bravery
Silver – Peace
White – Goodness
Yellow – Betrayal

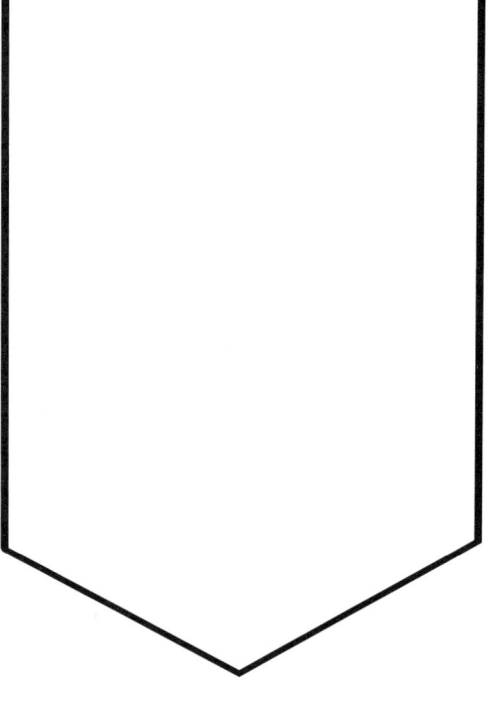

© Pieces of Learning

Maps, Graphs & Charts

Make a Map for Milo

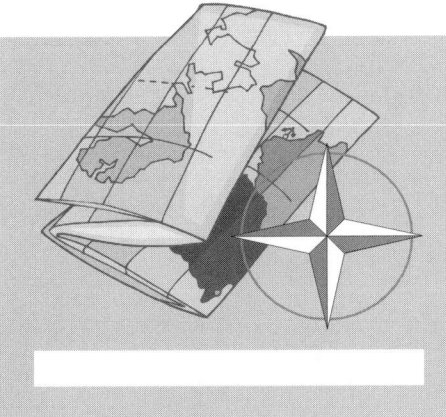

"... it was a beautiful map, in many colors, showing principal roads, rivers and seas, towns and cities, mountains and valleys, intersections and detours and sites of outstanding interest both beautiful and historic. The only trouble was that Milo had never heard of any of the places it indicated, and even the names sounded most peculiar."

- From the beginning of Milo's Adventures *The Phantom Tollbooth*

The Phantom Tollbooth
By Norton Juster
Illustrated by Jules Feiffer

STORY SYNOPSIS

The story of Milo, our young hero, is one of discovery through travel. Milo is insipidly drifting through life until the day he discovers a surprise package waiting for him in his apartment. This package includes a magic, genuine turnpike tollbooth, three precautionary signs, assorted coins, and one map "up to date and carefully drawn by master cartographers, depicting natural and man-made features and one book of traffic regulations." Because he has nothing better to do, he assembles the kit, travels though the tollbooth, and enters "The Lands Beyond." He soon acquires two traveling companions, Tock, a watchdog, and Humbug, a loquacious insect. The three travelers have many adventures as they travel through forests and over mountains. Milo returns home and discovers that only an hour has passed. He also learns that his journey has taught him much and provided a cure for his boredom.

CONTENT CONNECTION

Just as there are maps depicting J.R.R. Tolkien's Middle-earth, C.S. Lewis's Narnia, and Brain Jacques' Redwall Abby, Norton Juster has included a map of "The Lands Beyond" at the beginning of his entertaining *The Phantom Tollbooth*. While this map is obviously more concerned with showcasing word play than being an accurate rendition of an imaginary place, it does have many interesting features and is fun to study.

TIME REQUIRED: 25-30 minutes.

© Pieces of Learning

79

Maps, Graphs & Charts

Make a Map for Milo

OBJECTIVES
- The student will review the process of map reading.
- The student will identify the terms key/legend, compass rose, and scale.
- The student will complete a map labeling activity.
- The student may participate in the extension activity creating a map that represents a setting in a literary work.

MATERIALS
- Visuals - **How to Read a Map** (p.83) and **Candy Isle** (p.85)
- Activity Sheet - **Make a Map for Milo** (p.84) - one copy for each group or student
- Colored pencils and/or markers
- Optional – Copies of maps and atlases and a copy of *The Phantom Tollbooth* by Norton Juster for student inspection
- Optional - Extension Activity - **Atlas of imaginery Places** (p.82)

PROCEDURE

1. Prepare the visuals and activity sheets prior to class instruction.

2. Introduce the students to the lesson by telling them that they will be pretending to help a fictional character in today's lesson. Explain to them that Milo, from the book *The Phantom Tollbooth*, discovered an uncharted island during his visit to "The Lands Beyond" and they will be learning how to help him create a map of this sweet place, Candy Isle.

3. Display the visual and explain that a review about **How to Read a Map** is necessary before creating the map.

4. Read the five steps, referring to the very simple map on the bottom of the visual. Possible questions, comments, and observations might include:

   a. Identify the map's focus - The map's title will tell you its subject and the physical area it represents. **What is the map's title?** Book Island. **What physical area does it represent?** It is an imaginary island in the Read Sea.

   b. Study the key/legend - The key or legend on a map explains the identifying lines, symbols, colors, and shading used. **What two symbols are in the key?** An airplane represents the airport, and a tent stands for camping areas.

   c. Check directions - Maps often include a compass rose. This is the symbol and identifies north, south, east, and west. (If there is no compass rose assume that north is at the top of the map.) **Library Lake is in what part of Book Island?** The North.

80 © Pieces of Learning

Maps, Graphs & Charts

Make a Map for Milo

d. **Check distances** – Maps often include scales to help relate distances on the map to the actual area involved. **One unit on the scale is equal to how many miles?** 10 Miles. **Would you say that its widest section Book Island is nearer to 60 or 110 miles across?** [60]

e. **Look at the larger context** – The location of a specific place on earth can be determined by locating its latitude and longitude. **There are no lines of latitude or longitude on this map. Why do you think this is so?** The map is imaginary and does not represent an actual location.

5. Distribute **Make a Map for Milo** and writing tools. Students may work independently or in groups.

6. Instruct the students that they have about ten minutes to add the listed items to the map provided. Tell them that there is no right or wrong solution to the assignment and that each map will look different. Encourage creativity. (You may wish to keep the visual **How to Read a Map** displayed while the students work so they can use it as a reference.)

7. Check for understanding by displaying the Visual - **Candy Isle**.

EVALUATION

Maps filled in by the students will be unique to that student or group. However, the questions at the bottom of the visual will check for understanding and tie the lesson together.

- **Does your map look similar to this one?** *They will not look like the displayed map, and some students may need to be reassured this is just fine.*
- **How is it the same?** *The maps include the same information, some of it in the same place.*
- **How is yours different?** *The symbols and location of the specific places will be different.*
- **Which one do you like better?** *Students usually like their map best!*
- **Why?** *They like it because, if color pencils or markers were used, it is more colorful and attractive.*

EXTENSION

Creating maps is a passion for many visual/spatial learners. Encourage these students to draw and label maps of the imaginary settings they find in their favorite library books. The maps can be kept in a three ring binder for other students to view. This binder can be an *Atlas of Imaginary Places*.

© Pieces of Learning

Maps, Graphs & Charts

Make a Map for Milo

Atlas of Imaginary Places

Draw and label a map representing one of the imaginary places listed below. You may also know of another literary location that you would like to depict . . . or even create one of your own. Well-done, detailed maps will be placed in the library's *Atlas of Imaginary Places*.

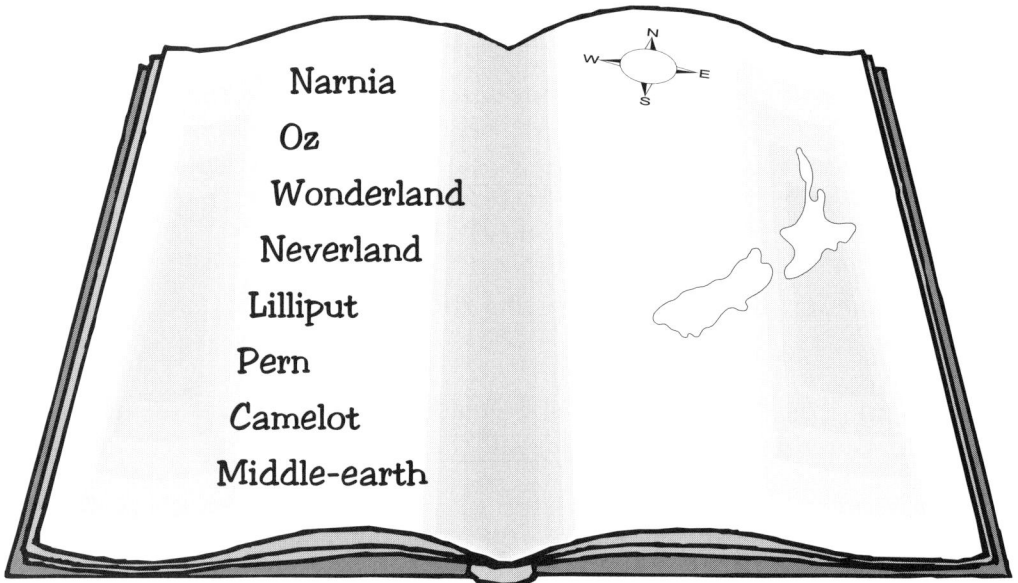

Narnia
Oz
Wonderland
Neverland
Lilliput
Pern
Camelot
Middle-earth

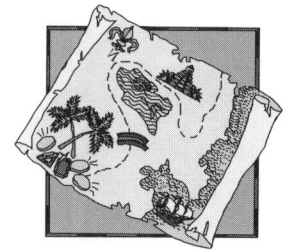

© Pieces of Learning

Maps, Graphs & Charts

Make a Map for Milo

How to Read a Map

1. Identify the map's focus - The map's title will tell you its subject and the physical area it represents.

2. Study the key/legend - The key or legend on a map explains the identifying lines, symbols, colors, and shading used.

3. Check directions - Maps often include a compass rose. This is the symbol and identifies north, south, east, and west. (If there is no compass rose assume that north is at the top of the map.)

4. Check distances – Maps often include scales to help relate distances on the map to the actual area involved.

5. Look at the larger context – The location of a specific place on earth can be determined by locating its latitude and longitude.

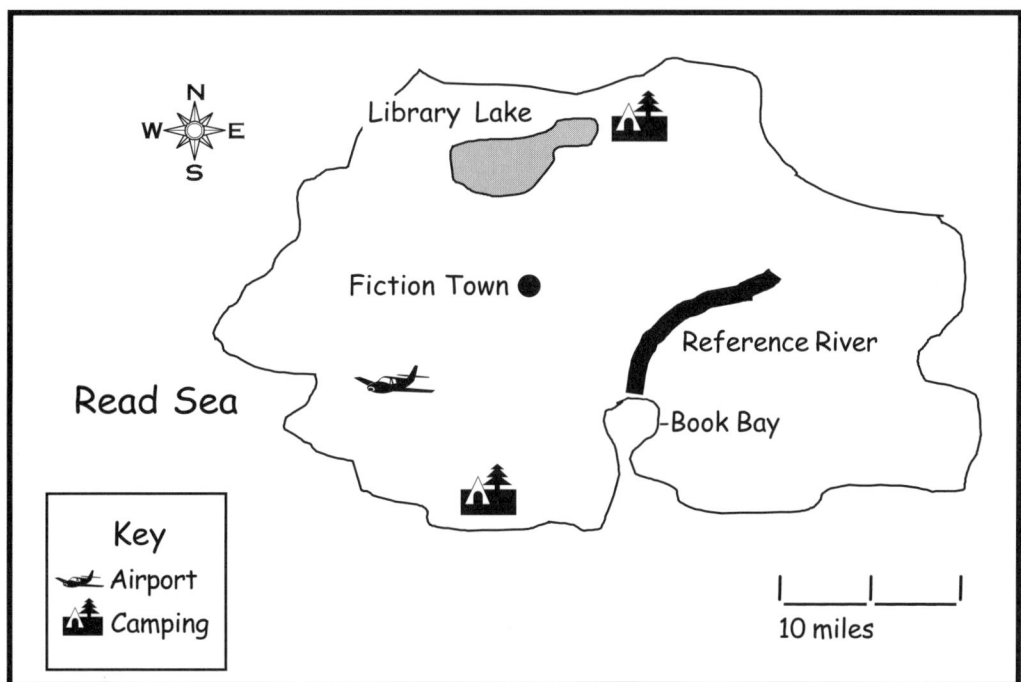

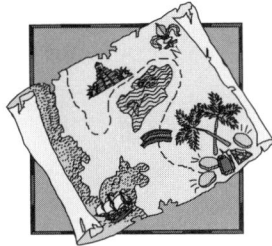

© Pieces of Learning

83

Maps, Graphs & Charts

Make a Map for Milo

Make a Map for Milo

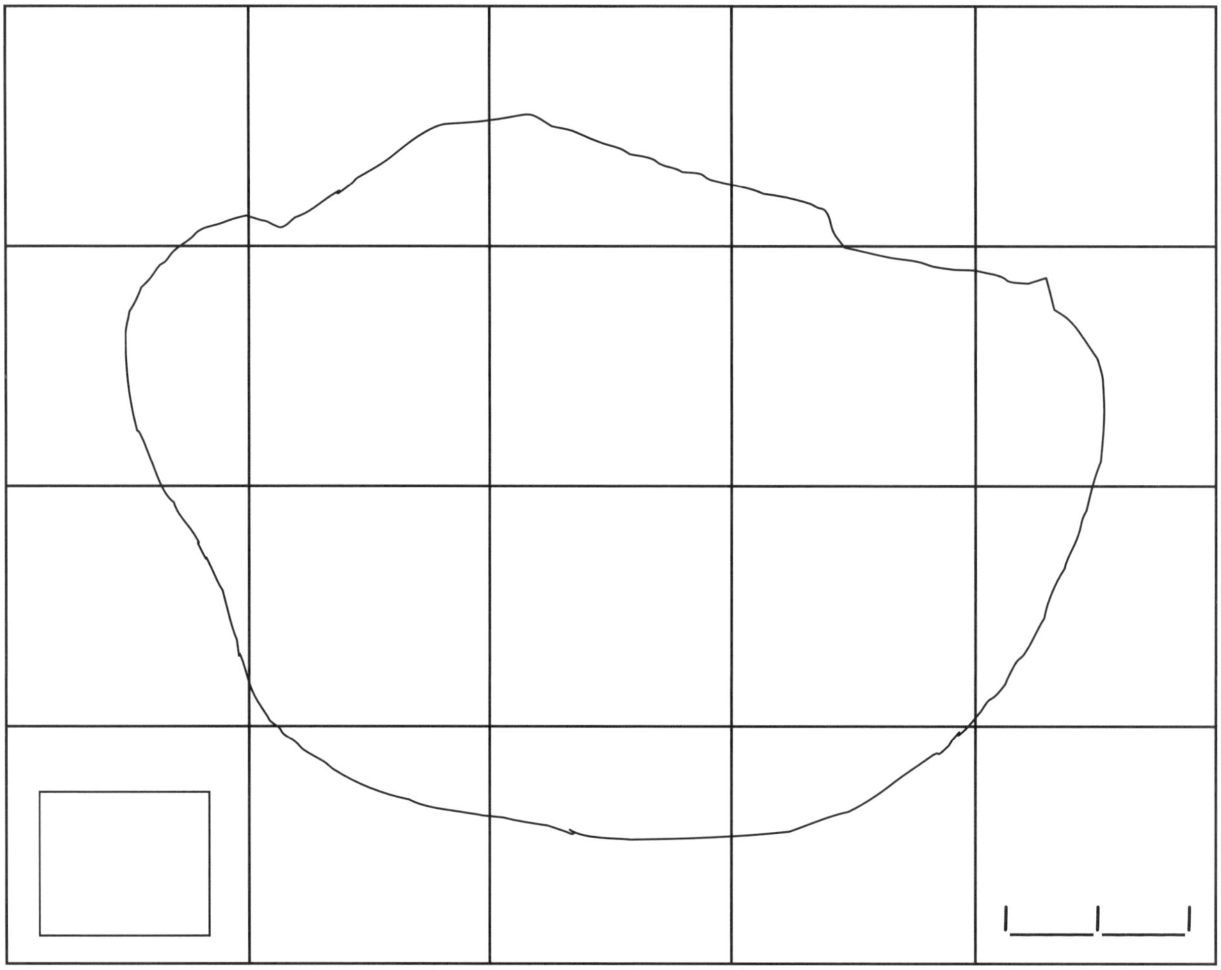

Directions - Add the following items to the map above.

   A title: Candy Isle (Candy Isle is located in the
       Sea of Knowledge)
   A compass rose
   A key – 3 symbols (Ice Cream Parlor, Sweet Shop, Bakery)
   2 Ice Cream Parlors, 1 Sweet Shop and 3 Bakeries
   A scale that shows one unit equals one mile
   A city, Sugar Town
   A river, Chocolate Syrup River

© Pieces of Learning

Maps, Graphs & Charts

Make a Map for Milo

Candy Isle

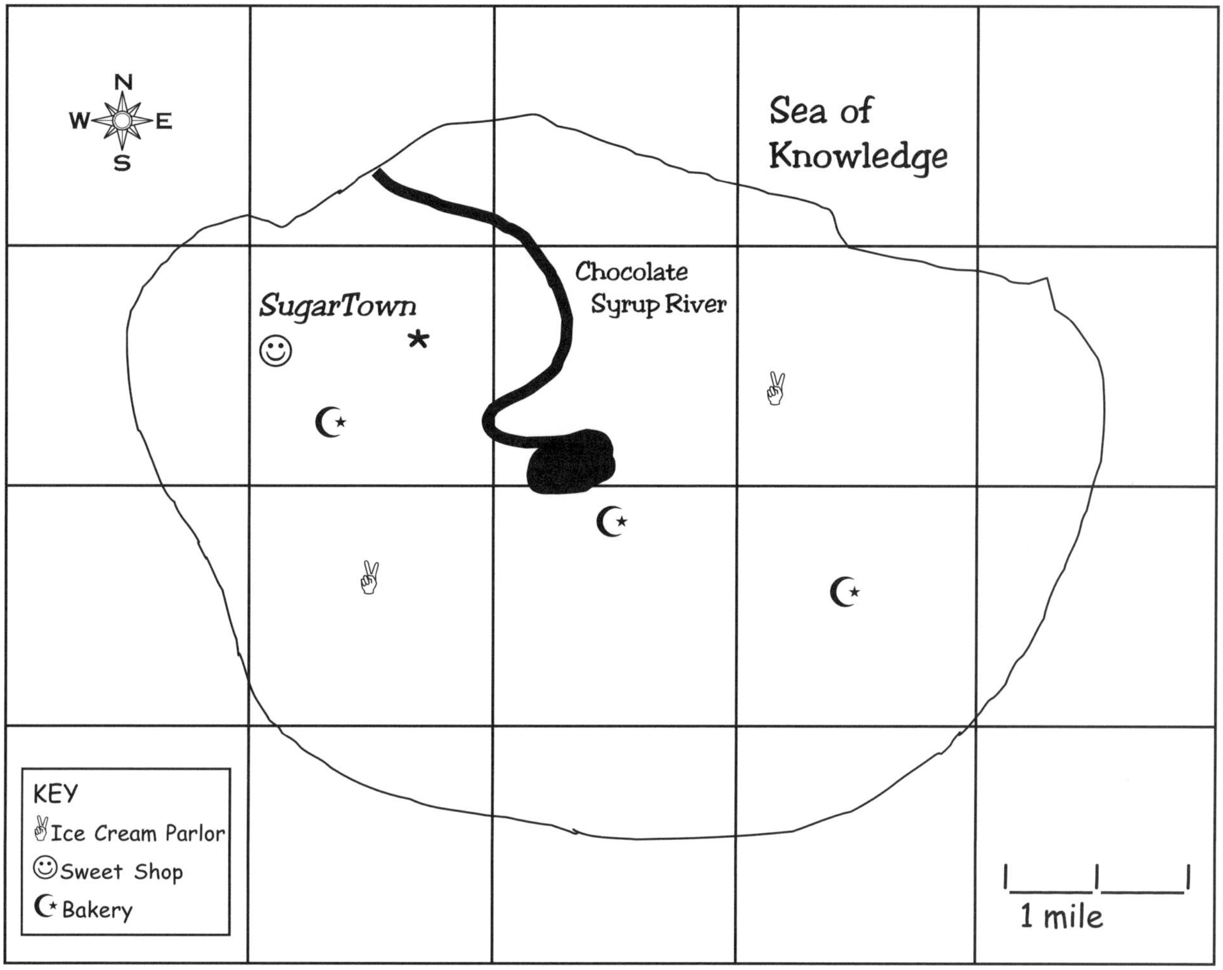

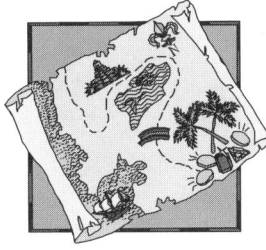

KEY
- ✌ Ice Cream Parlor
- ☺ Sweet Shop
- ☾★ Bakery

Sea of Knowledge

SugarTown

Chocolate Syrup River

1 mile

Does your map look similar to this one?

How is it the same?

How is yours different?

Which one do you like better? Why?

© Pieces of Learning

Maps, Graphs & Charts

Grid Work: Mapping a Serious Situation

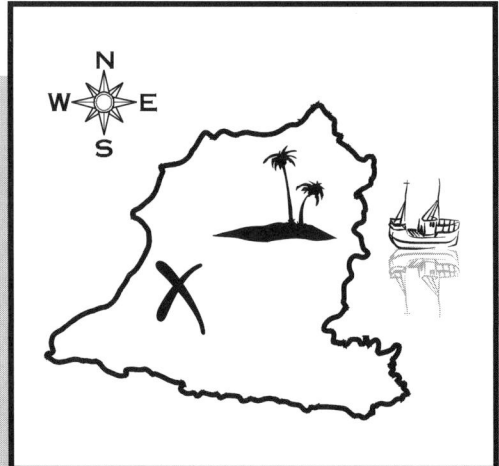

"There it is!" Violet pointed a finger at the tiny spot on the map marked Curdled Cave. "Directly across form Damocles Dock and just west of Lavender Lighthouse. Let's go!"

- Violet Baudelaire
A Series of Unfortunate Events: The Wide Window

A Series of Unfortunate Events
The Wide Window
Book the Third
By Lemony Snicket

STORY SYNOPSIS

Book three in the saga of the three wretched Baudelaire orphans finds them under the guardianship of their paranoid Aunt Josephine. It is not long before the evil Count Olaf, disguised as a one-eyed, peg-legged sailboat merchant, comes back on the scene. He is still trying to gain control of the surviving Baudelaires and their fortune. The children must use their wits . . . and an atlas to save themselves.

CONTENT CONNECTION

Violet, Klaus, and Sunny have decoded an encrypted message left by Aunt Josephine. Their fearful guardian is hiding in the Curdled Cave, and they are going to have to find her! The children know they will need an atlas and find one under a bed. Unfortunately, this book of maps has four hundred seventy-eight pages in it. The children quickly turn to the index, find the place they are searching for, and locate it on a map. Their knowledge of reference materials and map reading has helped them solve a problem. (The reader can count on the fact that they will soon encounter another, more precarious one!)

TIME REQUIRED: 30 minutes.

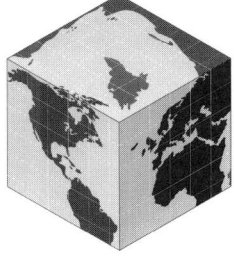

OBJECTIVES
- The student will use a grid to locate places on a map.
- The student will create and draw a map on a preexisting grid.
- The student may take a test for understanding.
- The student may participate in the extension activity dealing with maps and knowledge of literary works.

Maps, Graphs & Charts

Grid Work: Mapping a Serious Situation

MATERIALS
- Visual - **Grid Work: Mapping a Serious Situation** (p.89)
- Activity - **Grid Work: Mapping a Serious Situation** (p.90) - a copy for each student or group
- Water-soluble marker for transparency
- Colored pencils for student use
- Activity - **Grid Work: Mapping a Serious Situation - EVALUATION** (p.91)
- Optional: Various atlases for display and reference
- Optional: Copies of *Lemony Snicket's Series of Unfortunate Events* books for student check out

PROCEDURE

1. Prepare visual and activity sheets and collect materials prior to class.

2. Display the visual **Grid Work: Mapping a Serious Situation**. Tell the students that they will be working with mapping skills. Read the introduction.

3. Demonstrate to the students that the box Aunt Josephine's house may be found in box 4-B of the grid by placing your left finger on the letter B on the left side on the grid, the vertical line. Then place a right finger on house and move down to the number 4 on the bottom, the horizontal line.

4. Ask the questions located on the bottom of the visual.
   In what box is the compass rose located? **1-A**
   What is located in box 4-A? **The Lavender Lighthouse**
   In how many boxes can Damocles Dock be found? **Two, 4-C and 4-D**
   The Curdled Cave is located in what box? **2-B**
   In what box is the scale bar located? **5-D**
   Note: You may need to review with the student the terms **compass rose** (the part of a map that shows direction) and **scale bar** (the symbol used on a map to show distance).

5. Divide the students into groups. Distribute the activity sheet (p.90) and colored pencils or markers to each group. (Students may work individually.)

6. Read the directions on the top of the activity sheet and check for understanding. Encourage students to be creative.

7. Allow ten to fifteen minutes for the completion of the map.

8. Encourage students to share their solutions with the class.
   Optional: These maps make an attractive display for an interesting bulletin board.

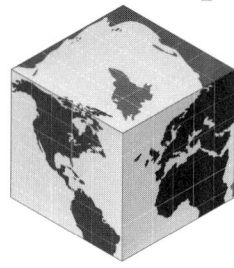

© Pieces of Learning

Maps, Graphs & Charts

Grid Work: Mapping a Serious Situation

EVALUATION

A tool for evaluation of student understanding has been included with this lesson. **Grid Work: Mapping a Serious Situation, EVALUATION** may be used by the resource teacher conducting the lesson or by the classroom teacher at a later date.

ANSWERS: PART I 1. B, 2. D, 3. E., 4. A, 5. B.   PART II Answers will vary.

EXTENSION

Advanced and/or very creative students may wish to have fun creating their own "Imaginary Literary Island."

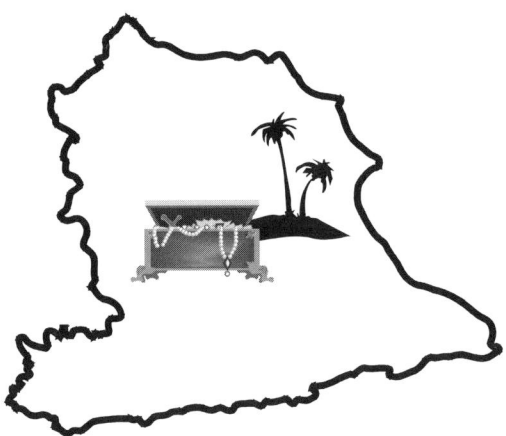

"Imaginary Literary Island"

Directions: Select a favorite story and create an island that is totally devoted to the plot, setting, and characters of that story located in the middle of an unknown ocean. For example, an island located in the Sweet Sea, may have a Marshmallow Mountain Range, Vanilla Valley, Bubble Gum Bay, and Candy Cove. (Did you guess the book in question was *Charlie and the Chocolate Factory* by Roald Dahl?)

Draw and label your map. Your creation must have at least ten locations, a compass rose, and a scale bar. Do not forget to name your island!

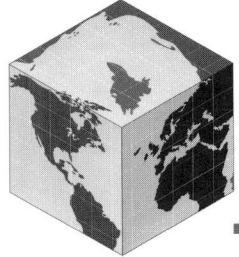

© Pieces of Learning

Maps, Graphs & Charts

Grid Work: Mapping a Serious Situation

A grid is a set of vertical and horizontal lines used to locate places on a map. Letters and numbers are used around the edges of the map to label the areas marked off by lines. For example, Aunt Josephine's house is located in box B-4.

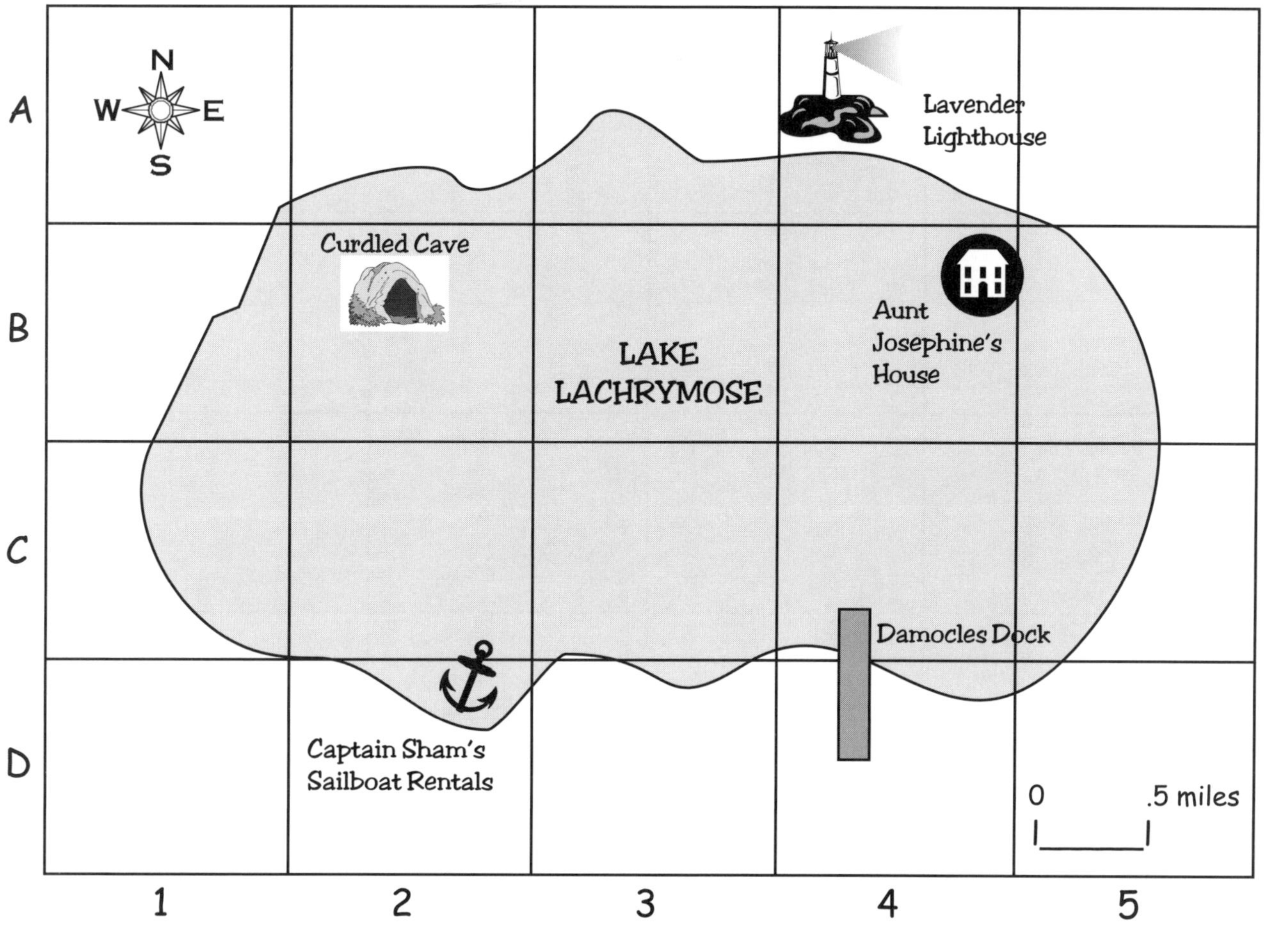

Questions:

In what box is the compass rose located? _____

What is located in box 4-A? _____

In how many boxes can Damocles Dock be found? _____

The Curdled Cave is located in what box? _____

In what box is the scale bar located? _____

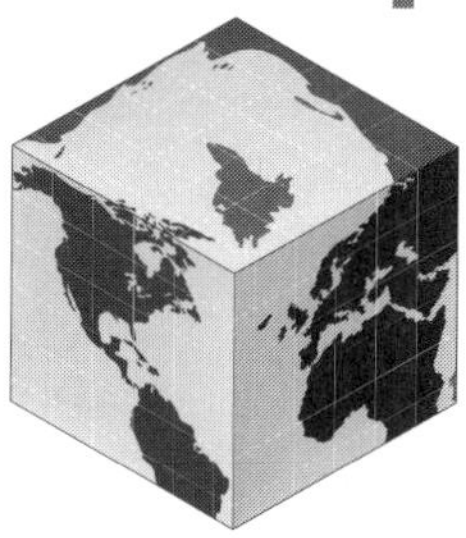

© Pieces of Learning

89

Maps, Graphs & Charts

Grid Work: Mapping a Serious Situation

Grid Work: Mapping a Serious Situation

Create your own "Imaginary Island." You <u>must</u> include the three places in the correct location listed in the Grid Index below. You may be creative with our other choices. Have fun!

Island Name: _____

	1	2	3	4
A				
B				
C				
D				

Index

Cave B-3   Your Choice _____   Your Choice _____

Swamp C-3   Your Choice _____   Your Choice _____

Volcano B-2 Your Choice _____   Your Choice _____

© Pieces of Learning

Maps, Graphs & Charts

Grid Work: Mapping a Serious Situation

Grid Work: Mapping a Serious Situation - Evaluation

PART I

Match the definition to the correct term

____ 1. Grid   A. The part of a map that shows direction
____ 2. Atlas   B. A set of lines used to find places on a map
____ 3. Index   C. The symbol used on a map to show distance
____ 4. Compass Rose   D. A book of maps
____ 5. Scale Bar   E. A list of names in alphabetical order

PART II

Directions Fill in the following on the grid below
- Label the vertical boxes with letters.
- Label the horizontal boxes with numbers.
- Draw and label a compass rose.
- Draw a scale bar.
- Make up, draw, and label at least five locations on the island. (This island is located in the Deep Blue Sea.)

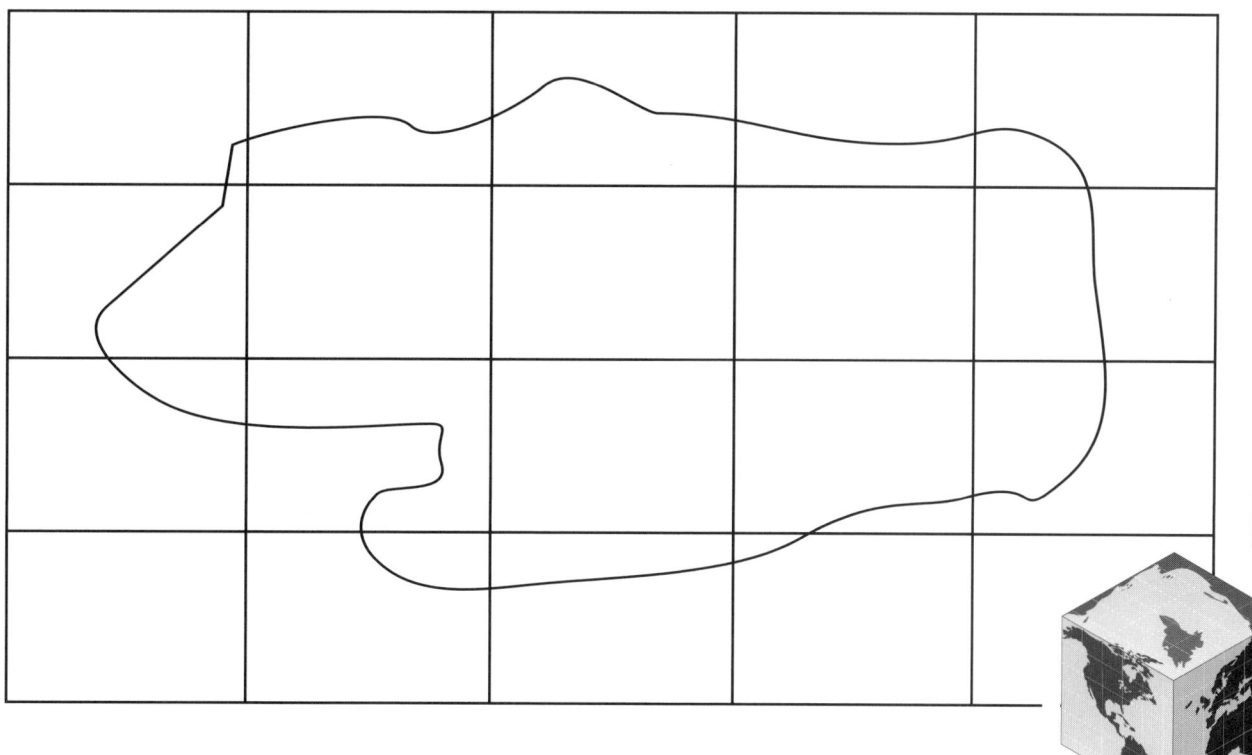

© Pieces of Learning

91

Maps, Graphs & Charts
Building Graphs

> *"Wayside School was accidentally built sideways. It was supposed to be only one story high, with thirty classrooms all in a row. Instead it is thirty stories high, with one classroom on each story. The builder said he was very sorry."*
>
> - Introduction
> *Sideways Stories From Wayside School*

Sideways Stories from Wayside School
By Lewis Sachar

STORY SYNOPSIS

Lewis Sachar's *Sideways Stories from Wayside School*, written decades before his award winning *Holes*, is a collection of thirty funny, strange, and engaging short stories. The characters in these tales are all students on the thirtieth floor of Wayside School. From the very beginning, when Mrs. Gorf ("frog" backwards) changes all of her students into apples, the reader realizes this is an out-of-the-ordinary place and that anything can happen here. Mrs. Jewls, sweet but not the brightest gem in the jeweler's tray, replaces Mrs. Gorf, and soon we are learning about Todd, D.J., Leslie, the three Erics, and all the other students in the class. Each story stands alone, contains a lesson of some sort, and makes a wonderful read aloud.

CONTENT CONNECTION

Mrs. Jewls teaches her students about addition, subtraction, and fractions in an interesting manner. She would probably do the same when teaching about graphs. Just like any other school, there are many things in Wayside School that can be tabulated when teaching a graphing lesson. However, dead rats are probably unique to the class on the thirtieth story. They keep trying to sneak into the room!

TIME REQUIRED: 30 minutes.

OBJECTIVES
- The student will interpret a bar graph.
- The student, using supplied data, will create a bar graph.
- The student will collect data to create a unique bar graph.
- The student may participate in a research extension activity dealing with mountain heights.

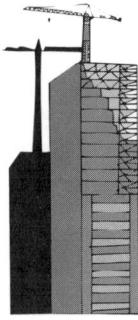

Maps, Graphs & Charts
Building Graphs

MATERIALS
- Visual - **Character Groups at a Glance** (p.95)
- Activity Sheet - **Building a Bar Graph** (p.96)
- Graph Paper (p.97)
- Rulers, pencils, markers, and other tools to help create a bar graph

PROCEDURE

1. Prepare visual and activity sheets and collect the materials prior to class.

2. Explain to the students that the data for the graph that will be in today's lesson was taken from the book *Sideways Stories form Wayside School* written by Louis Sachar. Tell the students that in this funny book, "Wayside School was accidentally built sideways. It was supposed to be only one story high, with thirty classrooms all in a row. Instead it is thirty stories high, with one classroom on each story. The builder said he was very sorry."

3. Display the visual **Character Groups at a Glance**. Read the introduction to the class. Solicit answers for the questions under the graph.
   How many teachers are represented on this graph? **2**   boys? **18**   girls? **15**
   dead rats? **3**

   Why do you think the number of students is marked in increments of 2?
   Possible Answers:
   It looks less cluttered that way. That is all that is needed. Half way up the column means one more.
   In what ways do think bar graphs can be useful?
   Possible Answers: *It is easy to compare things. Reading a graph is faster than reading a paragraph. Graphs are neat to look at.*
   Where would you find examples of bar graphs?
   Possible Answers: *Bar graphs can be found in math books and in science books. Newspapers and magazines use bar graphs. Television commercials show bar graphs sometimes.*

4. Distribute the activity sheet **Building a Bar Graph**. Review the directions with the students. Students may work individually or in groups.

5. Give each student or group graph paper, rulers, markers, etc.

6. Allow students 15 minutes to complete the bar graph.

7. Check for completeness and understanding.

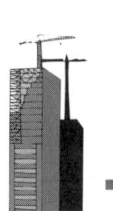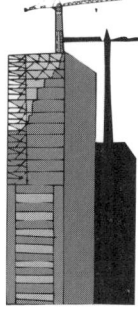

Maps, Graphs & Charts

Building Graphs

EVALUATION

The students' bar graphs should look "somewhat" similar to the one below. Note: This is a project where the process is more important that the product. However, the students may create some fairly impressive graphs. These display very well on bulletin boards.

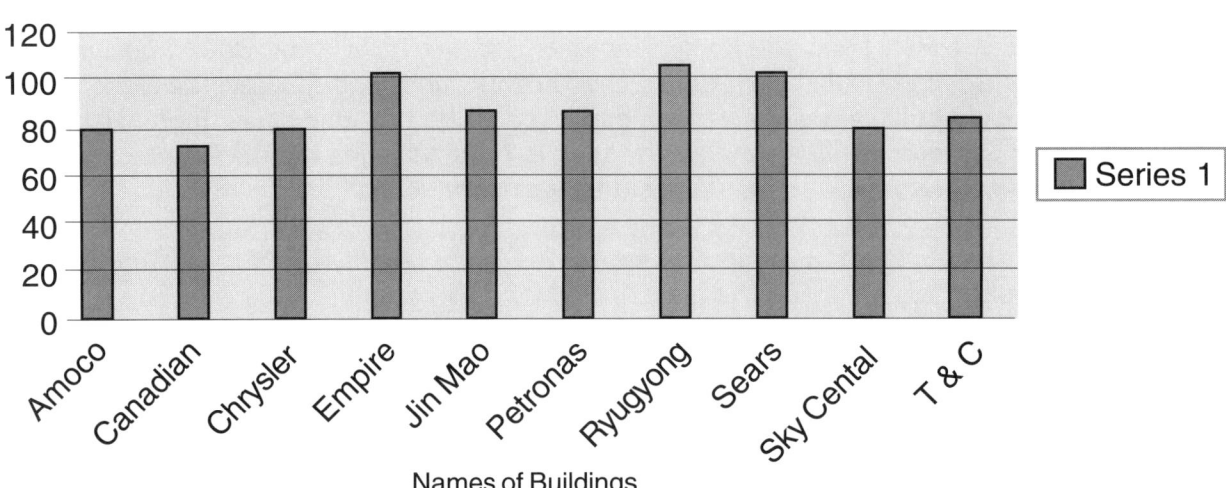

EXTENSION

To Great Heights!

Which mountains are the tallest in the world?

- Using an almanac, encyclopedia, or the Internet find the ten highest mountains in the world.

- Using this information create a bar graph, or any other type of graph, to give a visual picture of the results of your research.

- List five interesting facts concerning the results of your investigation.

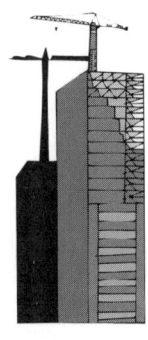

94 © Pieces of Learning

Maps, Graphs & Charts

Building Graphs

Character Groups at a Glance

Bar graphs are a convenient way to plainly show relationships between groups. In the bar graph below it is easy to see that there are more boy students in the class than there are girl students.

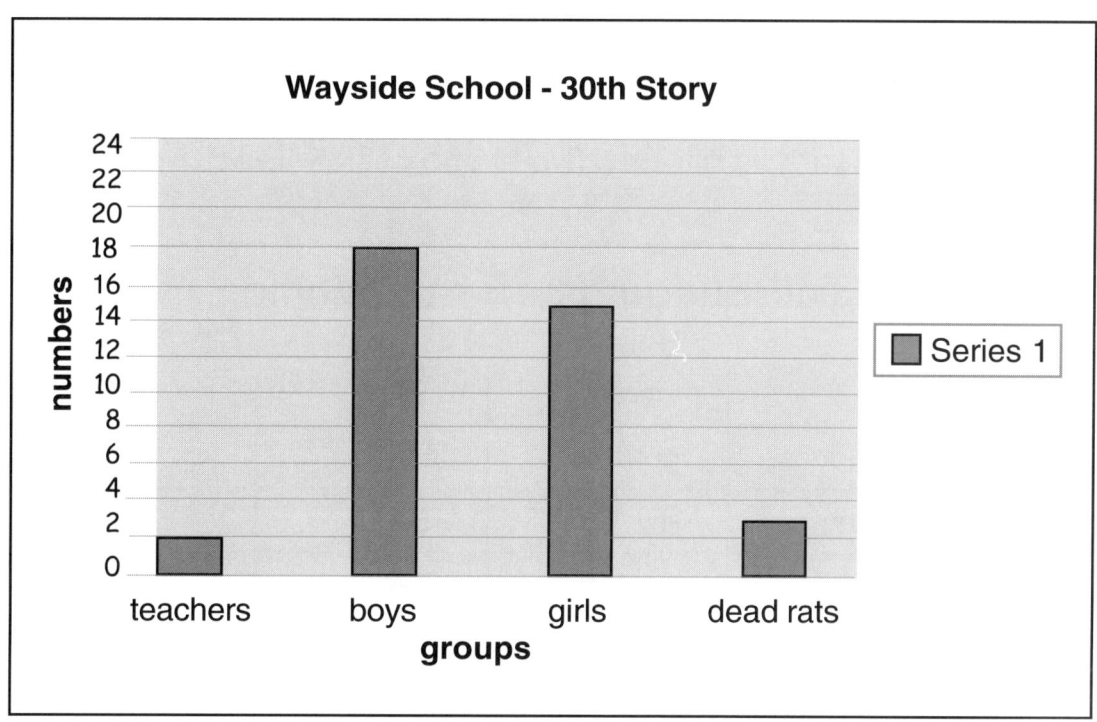

How many teachers are represented on this graph? boys? girls? dead rats?

Why do you think the number of students is marked in increments of 2?

In what ways do think bar graphs can be useful?

Where would you find examples of bar graphs?

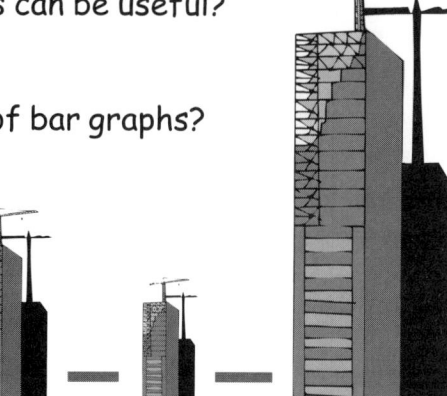
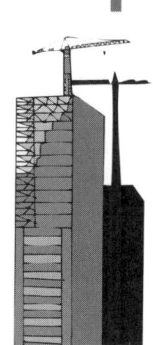

© Pieces of Learning

Maps, Graphs & Charts
Building Graphs

Building a Bar Graph

At thirty stories, Wayside School could be considered a very tall building. However, there are many taller buildings in the world. Below find a chart listing some EXTREMELY tall buildings. Using this information, graph paper, rulers and markers, make a bar graph that will compare the number of stories in each building.

INCLUDE:
- A Title
- Labels
- Numbers indicating increments. (Units of 5 or 10 will work well)
- Color and neatness

Tall Buildings of the World

Building Name	City	Country	Number of Stories
Amoco Building	Chicago	USA	80
First Canadian Place	Toronto	Canada	72
Chrysler Building	New York	USA	79
Empire State Building	New York	USA	102
Jin Mao Building	Shanghai	China	88
Petronas Twin Towers	Kuala Lumpur	Malaysia	88
Ryugyong Hotel	Pyongyang	North Korea	105
Sears Tower	Chicago	USA	102
Sky Central Plaza	Guangzhou	China	80
T & C Tower	Kaoshiung	Taiwan	85

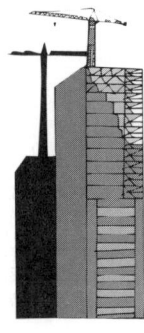

Maps, Graphs & Charts

Building Graphs

Graph Paper

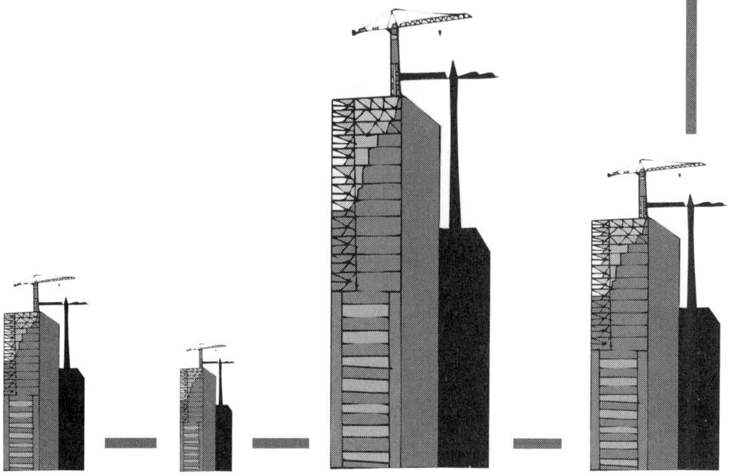

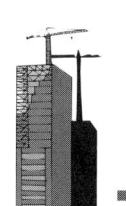

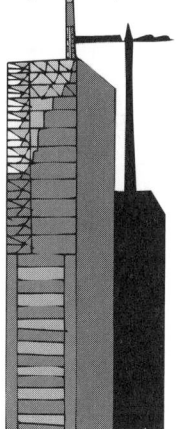
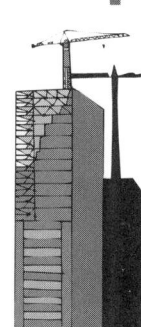

Maps, Graphs & Charts

Codes, Ciphers, and Secret Messages

> *"He held out a page for Sunny to see, and then pointed to the words 'Ana Gram.' "We thought this was someone's name," Klaus said, "but it's really a kind of code. An anagram is when you move the letters around in one or more words to make another word or words."*
>
> - Klaus Baudelaire
> Explaining a clue to Sunny
> A Series of Unfortunate Events

The Hostile Hospital
Book the Eighth
By Lemony Snicket

STORY SYNOPSIS

Things have gotten no better for the poor Baudelaire orphans in book eight in the *Series of Unfortunate Events* chronicles, *The Hostile Hospital*. Now accused of murder, their faces are on the front page of *The Daily Punctilio* for all to see. In fact, the newspaper has incorrectly reported the "death" of the evil Count. He is very much alive and still out to destroy the children and collect their fortune.

In their zeal to uncover the truth concerning the death of their parents, Violet, Klaus and Sunny find themselves in the records room of Heimlich Hospital. It is here that they discover the most important thing a hospital does is paper work. They also learn that much of the filing system is cryptic and that one needs to be a code breaker to understand the true meaning of what has been happening. However, before they can find the correct file and decode it, they are discovered. Soon they are devoting all of their efforts to avoiding the clutches of Count Olaf and his gang.

CONTENT CONNECTION

Written as a "tongue-in-cheek" melodrama, the stories by Lemony Snicket are very popular to a wide range of students. Reluctant readers enjoy the slapstick humor and the impossible predicaments the children must endure. Girls find a heroine in Violet and boys like the dumb adults and the baby who bites everything. Sophisticated readers love the word play, hidden messages and double meanings. Librarians and reading teachers think the well-read Klaus is a wonderful young man and a perfect role model.

One of the turning points in *The Hostile Hospital* is when Klaus and Sunny find they must decode an anagram in order to save Violet from getting a cranioectomy. (That's right, the removal of her head!) With the help of the letters in a can of alphabet soup they are able to decipher a hidden message and run to the rescue. The Baudelaire orphans have discovered that anagrams, ciphers and secret messages turn up where you least expect them and that it is important to know how to encode and decode them.

Xipan
Naxoaw
Xhtan

TIME REQUIRED: 30-35 minutes.

Maps, Graphs & Charts

Codes, Ciphers, and Secret Messages

OBJECTIVES
- The student will be introduced to the concept of codes and the function they play in literature and history.
- The student will use a chart to decode and encode a message.
- The student may participate in extension activities dealing with anagrams and/or a numerical code and math computation.

MATERIALS
- Visuals - **Codes, Ciphers, and Secret Messages** (p.101) and **Cipher System Grid** (p.102)
- Activity - **Cipher System Grid** (p.103) - one worksheet for each group or student
- Water soluble marker
- Pencils
- Optional - Extension Activities **Morse Math** (p.104) and **Anagrams** (p.105)

PROCEDURE

1. Prepare visuals and activity sheets before class.

2. Tell the students that today's lessons deals with codes and the decoding and encoding of messages. (You may need to define "encoding" as the process of converting a message into a code.)

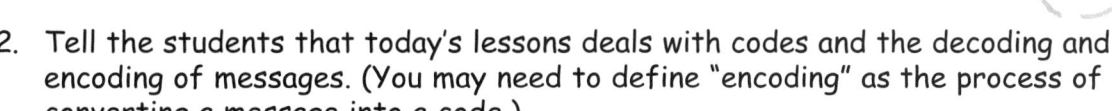

3. Display the visual **Codes, Ciphers and Secret Messages** and read it to the students. Encourage discussion from the class. Possible responses to the questions:
   Why do you think people use codes? *They have secrets. They do not what other people to know what they are writing. It is fun.*
   What part would a code play during a war? *A general does not what the enemy to know where the troops are. Surprise attacks are necessary.*
   Why do people like to decode messages? *They like to know secrets or they need the information that is in the code. Codes are like puzzles and people like to solve them.*
   What kind of stories would include coded secret messages? *Mystery stories and scary stories sometimes contain hidden messages. Sometimes travel and adventure stories have characters trying to decode messages.*

4. Display the visual **Cipher System Grid**. Read the directions and demonstrate the method used to identify the letter a number represents. Decode the message. Answer: CODES RULE!

5. Distribute activity sheet **Cipher System Grid** (p.103). Students may work independently or in groups. Encourage students who complete the activity quickly to create their own messages using the grid.

6. Check the activity as a group.

Xipan
Naxoaw
Xhtan

© Pieces of Learning 99

Maps, Graphs & Charts

Codes, Ciphers, and Secret Messages

EVALUATION

Answers for Activity sheet **Cipher System Grid**:

Decoded Message:

<u>S</u> <u>M</u> <u>O</u> <u>K</u> <u>E</u>   <u>S</u> <u>I</u> <u>G</u> <u>N</u> <u>A</u> <u>L</u> <u>S</u>   <u>A</u> <u>R</u> <u>E</u>
42 33 53 13 55   42 44 24 43 15 23 42   15 32 55

<u>C</u> <u>O</u> <u>D</u> <u>E</u> <u>D</u>   <u>M</u> <u>E</u> <u>S</u> <u>S</u> <u>A</u> <u>G</u> <u>E</u> <u>S</u>
35 53 45 55 45   33 55 42 42 15 24 55 42

Encode this message:

<u>42 34 44 12 42</u>   <u>15 52</u>   <u>42 55 15</u>   <u>35 15 43</u>   <u>11 42 55</u>   <u>52 34 55</u>
 S H I P S   A T   S E A   C A N   U S E   T H E

<u>44 43 52 55 32 43 15 52 44 53 43 15 23</u>   <u>14 23 15 24</u>   <u>35 53 45 55</u>
 I N T E R N A T I O N A L   F L A G   C O D E

<u>52 53</u>   <u>42 44 24 43 15 23</u>   <u>55 15 35 34</u>   <u>53 52 34 55 32</u>
 T O   S I G N A L   E A C H   O T H E R.

EXTENSION(S)

Two enrichment activities are included in this lesson. Students who are logical/mathematical learners will usually enjoy the **Morse Math** activity.

Answers:

1) ●●●●● + ●● --- = 7
2) ---●● − ●●●●● = 3
3) ● ---- + ●●●●- + ●● --- = 7
4) ----● − ●●● -- = 6
5) ●● --- X -●●●● = 12

The **Anagram** activity is especially challenging. Spatial/visual learners find it delightful; to others it can be frustrating. If this activity is set up as a center or an independent enrichment activity, it is helpful if the students have access to a set of letters for manipulation. The letters in a Scrabble Game work very well.

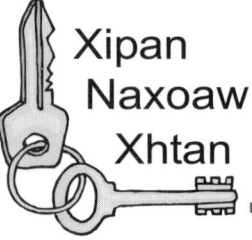

Xipan
Naxoaw
Xhtan

100   © Pieces of Learning

Maps, Graphs & Charts

Codes, Ciphers, and Secret Messages

Codes, Ciphers, and Secret Messages

Codes are everywhere. Bar codes on canned vegetables, in library books, and at the bottom of lottery tickets are good examples. The combination on a school locker is a code. The color-coded message of a traffic light is also one. Codes are methods of relaying information quickly or secretly.

A special kind of code is a cipher. Letters, words, or numbers are mixed up or substituted in this type of code. A cipher follows a specific key, or rule. It is necessary to know the key to understand the cipher.

Codes and ciphers have been used for a long time. The first codes used in ancient Egypt were probably created just for fun. Since then codes have been used all over the world and all through history.

For Discussion

Why do you think people use codes?

What part would a code play during a war?

Why do people like to decode messages?

What kind of stories would include coded secret messages?

48B98D12F

Xipan
Naxoaw
Xhtan

© Pieces of Learning

101

Maps, Graphs & Charts
Codes, Ciphers, and Secret Messages

Cipher System Grid

5	A	B	C	D	E
4	F	G	H	I	J
3	K	L	M	N	O
2	P	Q	R	S	T
1	U	V	W	X/Y	Z
	1	2	3	4	5

This code works like a grid on a map. The number 43 would stand for the letter N. This is figured out by <u>first</u> locating 4 on the **horizontal** row, **then** 3 on the **vertical** column, and finding the letter where these intersect.

Using this system, decode the following message:

$\overline{35}$ $\overline{53}$ $\overline{45}$ $\overline{55}$ $\overline{42}$ $\overline{32}$ $\overline{11}$ $\overline{23}$ $\overline{55}$!

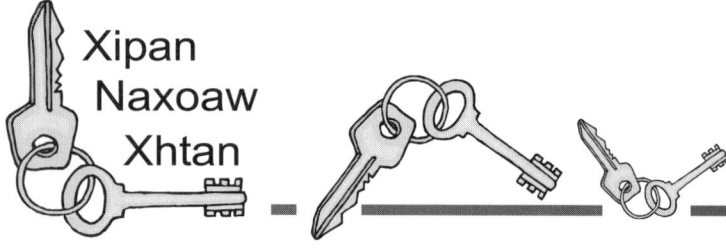

Xipan
Naxoaw
Xhtan

102

© Pieces of Learning

Codes, Ciphers, and Secret Messages

Cipher System Grid

5	A	B	C	D	E
4	F	G	H	I	J
3	K	L	M	N	O
2	P	Q	R	S	T
1	U	V	W	X/Y	Z
	1	2	3	4	5

This code works like a grid on a map. The number 43 would stand for the letter N. This is figured out by <u>first</u> locating 4 on the <u>horizontal</u> row, <u>then</u> 3 on the <u>vertical</u> column, and finding the letter where these intersect.

Decode this message:

S M O K E   S I G N A L S   A R E
42 33 53 13 55   42 44 24 43 15 23 42   15 32 55

C O D E D   M E S S A G E S
35 53 45 55 45   33 55 42 42 15 24 55 42

Encode this message:

42 34 44 12 42   15 52   42 55 15   35 15 43   11 42 55   52 34 55
 S H I P S   A T   S E A   C A N   U S E   T H E

44 43 52 55 32 43 15 52 44 53 43 15 23   14 23 15 24   35 53 45 55
 I N T E R N A T I O N A L   F L A G   C O D E

52 53   42 44 24 43 15 23   55 15 35 34   53 52 34 55 32
 T O   S I G N A L   E A C H   O T H E R

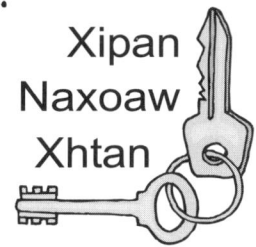

Xipan
Naxoaw
Xhtan

Maps, Graphs & Charts

Codes, Ciphers, and Secret Messages

EXTENSION 1

Morse Math

On May 24th 1843, in the Supreme Court Room in Washington, D.C. Samuel Morse transmitted the first telegraph message. This was accomplished by means of a code that uses groups of dots and dashes to stand for letters and numbers. These were turned into long and short electrical signals and sent along a telegraph wire. An operator at the other end of the wire decoded the message and sent one back.

Below find a chart with the Morse Code for numbers. Using this chart, solve the math problems.

1	● - - - -
2	● ● - - -
3	● ● ● - -
4	● ● ● ● -
5	● ● ● ● ●
6	- ● ● ● ●
7	- - ● ● ●
8	- - - ● ●
9	- - - - ●
0	- - - - -

1.) ● ● ● ● ● + ● ● - - - = _____

2.) - - - ● ● − ● ● ● ● ● = _____

3.) ● - - - - + ● ● ● ● - + ● ● - - - = _____

4.) - - - - ● − ● ● ● - - = _____

5.) ● ● - - - ✕ - ● ● ● ● = _____

Xipan
Naxoaw
Xhtan

Maps, Graphs & Charts

Codes, Ciphers, and Secret Messages

EXTENSION 2

Anagrams

In the book *The Hostile Hospital* by Lemony Snicket the children first think that Ana Gram is the name of a person. When they discover that an anagram is a code where letters of words are rearranged to form other words, they are able to figure out who is responsible for Violet's abduction and where she is being held.

For example, in the book the letters in COUNT OLAF have been rearranged to spell:

Playwright Al Funcoot
Dr. Flacutono
Dr. O. Lucafont
Dr. Tocuna *& Nurse* Flo

Can you change your name into another name or saying by using all the letters in your name?

-OR-

You may wish to experiment with names in history.
For Example:

Pocahontas = **Hot Soap Can**

Daniel Boone = **One Bone Laid**

Xipan
Naxoaw
Xhtan

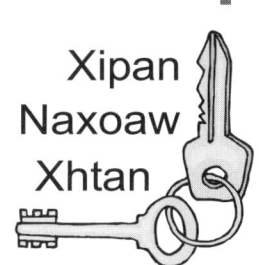

© Pieces of Learning

Maps, Graphs & Charts

The Time Warp Trio Timeline

> *"I swear I put The Book away in a safe spot so we wouldn't get time traveled into any more trouble. Maybe he isn't a real gladiator, and maybe this isn't Rome two thousand years ago."*
>
> – Joe, the narrator for the Time Warp Trio
> *See You Later, Gladiator*

See You Later, Gladiator
The Time Warp Trio Series
By Jon Scieszka

STORY SYNOPSIS

Once again, our three young heroes have been transported into the past. This event happens as result of a special book given to Joe by his uncle, a magician, as a birthday present. It seems as if *The Book* has the power to turn people into time travelers. This time, Joe and his friends Fred and Sam find themselves at the Colosseum in Rome fighting gladiators.

CONTENT CONNECTION

Jon Scieszka writes exciting fantasy books that have a special appeal to boys who tend to be reluctant readers. The main characters in these books are three guys who find themselves in unusual situations. The plots of these books are action packed, the dialog is snappy, and the historic facts basically accurate. Because the boy's adventures do not take place in chronological order, the series is ideal to use for teaching an introductory lesson concerning timelines.

TIME REQUIRED: 30-35 minutes.

OBJECTIVES
- The student will be introduced to the concept of timelines.
- The student will complete an activity placing historic events in chronological order.
- The student will construct and illustrate a foldable timeline.
- The student may participate in the extension activity dealing with a specific timeline.

MATERIALS
- Visual – **The Time Warp Trio Timeline** (p.109)
- Water soluble marker
- Activity sheets – **History Images** (p.110)
- Activity Sheet – **Time Warp Trio Timeline** (p.111)
- Scissors, glue/tape, pencils, and markers
- Optional – copies of Joe Scieszka's *Time Warp Trio* Books

Maps, Graphs & Charts

The Time Warp Trio Timeline

PROCEDURE

1. Prepare the visual and gather materials prior to class.

2. Introduce the lesson by informing the students they will be making their own time line. Define a time line as "A type of chart that divides periods of time to show a sequence of events."

3. Display the visual **The Time Warp Trio Timeline**. Read the introduction to the class. Complete the matching activity as a group. Answers:
   Book 1 *Knights of the Kitchen Table* **The Middle Ages 1000 A.D.**
   Book 3 *The Good, the Bad and the Goofy* **American Wild West, Mid 19th Century A.D.**
   Book 4 *Your Mother Was a Neanderthal* **Stone Age 70,000 B.C.**
   Book 5 *2095* **The Future**
   Book 6 *Tut Tut* **Ancient Egypt 1350 B.C.**
   Book 8 *It's All Greek to Me* **The Golden Age of Greece 400 B.C.**
   Book 9 *See You Later Gladiator* **Roman Empire 100 B.C.**
   Book 12 *Viking It and Liking It* **Norse Exploration 900 A.D.**
   Book 14 *Da Wild, Da Crazy, Da Vinci* **The Renaissance 16th Century A.D.**

4. Keep the visual displayed throughout the activity. However, cover up the top section, **Book Title**, leaving only the **Historical Time Periods** visible. Students may become confused as to the correct order of events if both lists are displayed.

5. Give each student or group scissors, glue/tape, pencils, and/or markers

6. Distribute **Time Warp Trio Timeline**. Instruct the students to cut out the large rectangle, and then fold on the dotted line. They are to then cut the horizontal lines. This creates little doors that may be opened separately. (It is helpful if there is an example of a completed time line for the students to see.)

7. Distribute the **History Images** activity sheet. Explain to the students that they will be creating a time line in which an image clue is on the front and the general time period of this historical period is hidden behind the image. (You may wish to tell the students that this is a good method of studying facts for a test.)

8. Instruct the students to color, cut out, and affix the images to the front of the folded tabs in the order listed on the displayed visual. Remind the students the images are not in order. They will need to use their knowledge to assign the correct image to the appropriate time period.

9. Inform the students that they are to write the corresponding time period behind the "door." Therefore, when the "door" is opened, this information will be revealed. **Note:** Students who complete this project early may wish to try to memorize the dates of the time periods, using their newly constructed time line as a study aid.

© Pieces of Learning

Maps, Graphs & Charts

The Time Warp Trio Timeline

EVALUATION
The completed time line should resemble this.

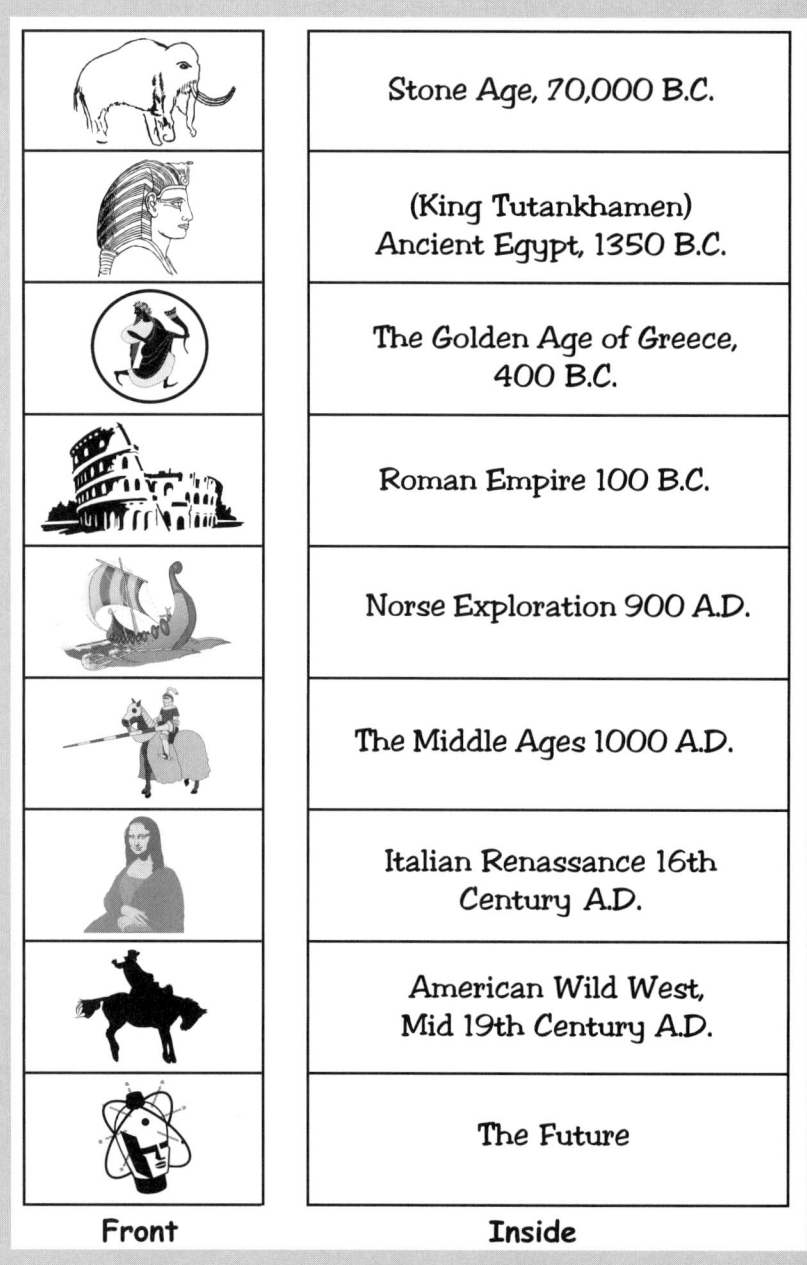

Front	Inside
🐘	Stone Age, 70,000 B.C.
👤	(King Tutankhamen) Ancient Egypt, 1350 B.C.
🏺	The Golden Age of Greece, 400 B.C.
🏛	Roman Empire 100 B.C.
⛵	Norse Exploration 900 A.D.
🐎	The Middle Ages 1000 A.D.
🖼	Italian Renassance 16th Century A.D.
🤠	American Wild West, Mid 19th Century A.D.
⚛	The Future

EXTENSION
Students who enjoy this type of activity may wish to make a detailed time line of a specific era, or one of a family member, or maybe even of their own life. Provide materials, paper, scissors, glue, markers, etc. at a center for students who wish to create a unique time line of their own.

Maps, Graphs & Charts

The Time Warp Trio Timeline

The Time Warp Trio Timeline

The "Time Travel" adventures of Fred, Joe, and Sam, by Jon Scieszka, are written in a funny and informative manner. However, they were not written in chronological sequence. (This means that the boys move through time in random order.)

Directions: Using the titles as hints, match the book title to the most logical period in history the boys will be visiting. Write the time period in the blanks following the titles.

Book Title

Book 1 *Knights of the Kitchen Table* _____

Book 3 *The Good, the Bad and the Goofy* _____

Book 4 *Your Mother Was a Neanderthal* _____

Book 5 *2095* _____

Book 6 *Tut Tut* _____

Book 8 *It's All Greek to Me* _____

Book 9 *See You Later Gladiator* _____

Book 12 *Viking It and Liking It* _____

Book 14 *Da Wild, Da Crazy, Da Vinci* _____

> **Historical Time Periods**
> Stone Age, 70,000 B.C.
> (King Tutankhamen) Ancient Egypt, 1350 B.C.
> The Golden Age of Greece, 400 B.C.
> Roman Empire 100 B.C.
> Norse Exploration 900 A.D.
> The Middle Ages 1000 A.D
> Renaissance 16th Century A.D.
> American Wild West, Mid 19th Century A.D.
> The Future

© Pieces of Learning

Maps, Graphs & Charts

The Time Warp Trio Timeline

History Images

110 © Pieces of Learning

Maps, Graphs & Charts

The Time Warp Trio Timeline

Time Warp Trio Timeline

Booklist

Charlie and the Chocolate Factory by Roald Dahl. Puffin Books, 1964.

Gulliver's Stories: Retold from Jonathan Swift by Edward W. Dolch, Marguerite Dolch, and Beulah Jackson. Scholastic Inc, 2001, c1961.

Harry Potter and the Order of the Phoenix by J.K. Rowling. Scholastic Inc., 2003.

Harry Potter and the Prisoner of Azkaban by J.K. Rowling. Scholastic Inc., 1999.

Harry Potter and the Sorcerer's Stone by J.K. Rowling. Scholastic Inc., 1997.

The Hostile Hospital by Lemony Snicket. Scholastic Inc., 2001.

I Was A Rat! by Philip Pullman. Dell Yearling, 2002.

The Lord of the Rings: The Fellowship of Ring by J.R.R. Tolkien. Ballantine Books, 1965.

The Lion, the Witch and the Wardrobe by C.S. Lewis. HarperCollins, 1950.

Peter Pan by J.M. Barrie. Scholastic Inc., 2002.

The Phantom Tollbooth by Norton Juster. Dell Yearling, Random House, 1989.

Sideways Stories from Wayside School by Lewis Sachar. Avon, 1978.

The Time Warp Trio: See You later, Gladiator by Jon Scieszka. Viking Penguin, 2000.

The Wide Window by Lemony Snicket. Scholastic Inc., 2001.

The Wonderful Wizard of Oz by Frank L. Baum. Harper Collins, 1987. (Originally published by Geo-M-Hill Co. in 1900)

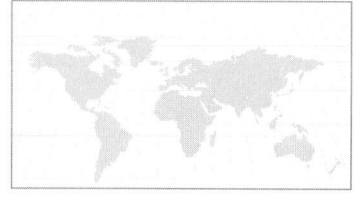